D0407393

WITHDRAWN
UTSA LIBRARIES

RENEWALS 458-4574

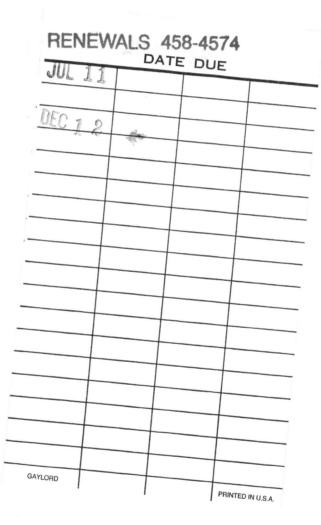

DATE DUE

JUL 11			
DEC 1 2			
GAYLORD			
			PRINTED IN U.S.A.

Environmental Warfare
A Technical, Legal and Policy Appraisal

sipri

Stockholm International Peace Research Institute

SIPRI is an independent institute for research into problems of peace and conflict, especially those of arms control and disarmament. It was established in 1966 to commemorate Sweden's 150 years of unbroken peace.

The institute is financed by the Swedish Parliament. The staff, the Governing Board and the Scientific Council are international.

Governing Board

Rolf Björnerstedt, Chairman (Sweden)
Egon Bahr (FR Germany)
Francesco Calogero (Italy)
Tim Greve (Norway)
Max Jakobson (Finland)
Karlheinz Lohs (German Democratic Republic)
Emma Rothschild (United Kingdom)
The Director

Director

Frank Blackaby (United Kingdom)

sipri

Stockholm International Peace Research Institute
Bergshamra, S-171 73 Solna, Sweden
Cable: Peaceresearch Stockholm
Telephone: 468-55 97 00

Environmental Warfare
A Technical, Legal and Policy Appraisal

Edited by
Arthur H. Westing

sipri

Stockholm International Peace Research Institute

Taylor & Francis
London and Philadelphia
1984

UK	Taylor & Francis Ltd, 4 John St, London WC1N 2ET
USA	Taylor & Francis Inc., 242 Cherry St, Philadelphia, PA 19106–1906

Copyright © SIPRI 1984

All rights reserved. No part of this publication may be reproduced, stored in a retrieval system, or transmitted, in any form or by any means, electronic, electrostatic, magnetic tape, mechanical, photocopying, recording or otherwise, without the prior permission of the copyright owner and publishers.

British Library Cataloguing in Publication Data

Environmental warfare.
   1. Weather Control—War use
   1. Westing, Arthur H. II. Stockholm International Peace
Research Institute
   358′.3   UG467

   ISBN 0-85066-278-8

Cover design by Malvern Lumsden
Typeset by Georgia Origination, Liverpool L3 9EG
Printed in Great Britain by Taylor & Francis (Printers) Ltd,
Basingstoke, Hants.

LIBRARY
The University of Texas
At San Antonio

Environmental Warfare: a Technical, Legal and Policy Appraisal is an outgrowth of a select symposium convened in Geneva on 24–27 April 1984 by the Stockholm International Peace Research Institute (SIPRI) together with the United Nations Institute for Disarmament Research (UNIDIR) and in co-operation with the United Nations Environment Progamme (UNEP). The present volume was prepared by SIPRI as a project within the SIPRI/UNEP programme on 'Military activities and the human environment'.

Preface

This book examines environmental warfare in its technical, legal and policy aspects. In the process, it provides a critical analysis of the 1977 Convention on the Prohibition of Military or any other Hostile Use of Environmental Modification Techniques (the Enmod Convention). It is sometimes argued that the Enmod Convention prevents the military from doing what it had no intention of doing anyway. However, to the extent that this is true, it is still a service to humanity to block off from military exploitation any part of the environment, no matter how remote the possibility of military use might seem at the moment, for in the future it might be less remote. There are many things that the military is doing now which were inconceivable 50 years ago.

The book will, it is hoped, contribute to the discussion which should be stimulated by the first review conference of the Enmod Convention, to be held in Geneva in September 1984. There is a growing concern throughout the world with environmental questions, and it is important that there should be an impenetrable barrier, set up for all time, preventing any military manipulation of the forces of nature.

SIPRI welcomed the opportunity to carry out this project in co-operation with the United Nations Institute for Disarmament Research (UNIDIR). This book is the second product of a research programme on military activities and the human environment, financed jointly by SIPRI and the United Nations Environment Programme (UNEP). It was edited by Professor Arthur H. Westing (of Hampshire College and SIPRI), who is an international authority on the ecological impact of war.

SIPRI   *Frank Blackaby*
May 1984   Director

Acknowledgements

The editor is pleased to acknowledge the very able research assistance of Carol Stoltenberg-Hansen, editorial assistance of Connie Wall and secretarial assistance of Deborah Flynn-Danielsson.

vii

Contents

Glossary and units of measure

I. *Glossary*

Atmosphere: The gaseous mass enveloping the Earth, including the particulate (solid and liquid) matter suspended in it; a component of the environment (*q.v.*).

Biosphere: The living component of the environment (*q.v.*), i.e., all of the biota (flora and fauna).

CCD: Conference of the Committee on Disarmament (Geneva); progenitor of the Conference on Disarmament (CD).

Enmod: Environmental modification (i.e., environmental manipulation).

Enmod Convention: Convention on the Prohibition of Military or any other Hostile Use of Environmental Modification Techniques of 1977 (see appendix 2).

Environment: The whole complex of conditions and forces that surround and can act upon an organism or community of organisms, including climatic, edaphic (soil), hydrological, biotic and artefactual (anthropogenic) factors; it includes the atmosphere, geosphere (lithosphere plus hydrosphere) and biosphere (*q.v.*).

Environment, human: The environment (*q.v.*) in which the organism or community of organisms that provides the focal point is *Homo sapiens*.

Environment, natural: The environment (*q.v.*) exclusive of anthropogenic factors.

Environmental warfare: warfare in which the environment (*q.v.*) is manipulated for hostile military purposes (see also chapter 1, section I).

Geneva Protocol I: Protocol I Additional to the Geneva Conventions of 1949, and Relating to the Protection of Victims of International Armed Conflicts of 1977 (see appendix 3).

Geosphere: The Earth, including the lithosphere and hydrosphere; a component of the environment (*q.v.*).

Hydrosphere: The liquid part of the Earth, i.e., the oceans; together with the lithosphere, making up the geosphere; a component of the environment (*q.v.*).

Lithosphere: The solid part of the Earth; together with the hydrosphere, making up the geosphere; a component of the environment (*q.v.*).

SIPRI: Stockholm International Peace Research Institute.

UNEP: United Nations Environment Programme (Nairobi).

UNIDIR: United Nations Institute for Disarmament Research (Geneva).

II. Units of measure

The units of measure and prefixes (and the abbreviations) employed in the text are in accordance with the international system (SI) of units (Goldman and Bell, 1981). Those mentioned in the text follow:

are (a) = 100 square metres = 1 076.39 square feet.

day (d) = 24 hours = 86 400 seconds.

degree Celsius (°C) = 1 kelvin (K). To convert temperature in degrees Celsius to temperature in degrees Fahrenheit, multipy by 1.8 and then add 32.

giga- (G-) = $10^9 \times$.

gram (g) = 10^{-3} kilogram = $2.204\,62 \times 10^{-3}$ pound.

hectare (ha) = 10^4 square metres = 0.01 square kilometre = 2.4751 05 acres.

hect(o)- (h-) = $100 \times$.

hour (h) = 3 600 seconds.

joule (J) = 0.238 846 calorie.

kilo- (k-) = $10^3 \times$.

kilogram (kg) = 2.204 62 pounds.

kilometre (km) = 10^3 metres = 0.621 371 mile.

kilometre, square (km^2) = 100 hectares = 247.105 acres = 0.386 102 square mile.

kiloton (kT) = 4.187×10^{12} joules, referring to the energy yield of a nuclear bomb; see also 'megaton'.

litre (L) = 10^{-3} m^3 = 0.264 172 US gallon = 0.219 969 British gallon.

mega- (M-) = $10^6 \times$.

megaton (MT) = 4.187×10^{15} joules, referring to the energy yield of a nuclear bomb; see also 'kiloton'.

metre (m) = 3.280 84 feet.

metre, cubic (m^3) = 10^3 litres = 264.172 US gallons = 219.969 British gallons = 1.307 951 cubic yards.

micro- (μ-) = $10^6 \times$.

second (s): see Goldman and Bell (1981, page 3).

Tera- (T-) = $10^{12} \times$.

ton (T): see 'kiloton' and 'megaton'.

watt (W) = joule per second. The designation 'e', as in W(e), indicates that the energy is in the form of electricity.

Reference

Goldman, D. T. and Bell, R.J. (eds). 1981. *International System of Units (SI)*. Washington: US National Bureau of Standards Special Publ. No. 330, 48 pp.

Introduction

Revulsion against the use of chemical weapons during World War I ultimately precipitated their proscription through the instrument of the Geneva Protocol of 1925. The horror engendered by the attempts to exterminate selected religious and ethnic groups during World War II led in time to the Genocide Convention of 1948. Outrage at the attempts to harness the forces of nature for hostile purposes during the Second Indochina War soon found expression in the Environmental Modification (Enmod) Convention of 1977, a major focus of this book.

Environmental warfare—warfare in which the environment is manipulated for hostile military purposes—has been a malevolent, though largely ineffectual, military desire throughout history. The two major forms of pent-up energy in the environment that have in the past been available for exploitation by the military commander are (*a*) the fuel represented by forest or other vegetation and (*b*) the potential energy of bodies of water held in check by levees or other barriers. Under special conditions, the former can be released by fire and the latter by breaching the barrier.

Only now are we perhaps on the threshold of developing the more sophisticated technical ability to control atmospheric, tectonic and biotic factors of the environment for effective hostile military purposes. Indeed, the Second Indochina War provides us with two examples (albeit, more or less feeble ones) of hostile manipulations of the environment that rely upon modern technology: in the first of these, the biotic component of the regional environment was disrupted through the application of plant poisons (herbicides) and by other means; and in the second, attempts were made to disturb the regional weather pattern through cloud seeding. The attempt at biotic disruption was by some standards successful, but in general required a massive, long-sustained effort for its accomplishment; the attempt at weather disruption was a failure despite a similarly substantial, long-sustained effort.

This book begins with a broad technical overview of environmental warfare—past, present and future—irrespective of the applicability of the Enmod Convention or other treaty (chapter 1). The term 'environment' is here taken to encompass both its natural and artefactual components (see glossary). The book goes on with scientific analyses of present and expected future capabilities regarding manipulation of the atmosphere (chapter 2) and of the geosphere (chapter 3). These reviews of present and expected capabilities in harnessing the forces of nature are followed by a broad examination of the development of international law regarding environmental disruption by military means (chapter 4). The relevance to arms control issues of the profoundly adverse impact of nuclear war on the regional and even global environment is developed as well (chapter 4).

The foregoing presentations set the stage for a searching analysis of the Enmod Convention, in anticipation of the first (five-year) review conference, to be held in September 1984. All of the essential provisions are analysed (chapter 5) and the particular question of verification is singled out as well (chapter 6). The book closes with a series of policy recommendations regarding environmental warfare in general and the Enmod Convention in particular (chapter 7).

The book is an outgrowth of a select symposium convened in Geneva on 24–27 April 1984, by SIPRI together with UNIDIR and in co-operation with UNEP.[1] The authors of the book are:

Professor *Richard A. Falk* (Department of Politics, Princeton University, Princeton, NJ 08540, USA), an authority on international law and policy.

Mr *Jozef Goldblat* (Stockholm International Peace Research Institute, Bergshamra, S-171 73 Solna, Sweden), an authority on arms-control law and policy.

Professor *Allan S. Krass* (School of Natural Science, Hampshire College, Amherst, MA 01002, USA. At SIPRI 1983–84), an authority on science and public policy.

Dr *Ernö Mészáros* (Institute for Atmospheric Physics, PO Box 39, H-1675 Budapest, Hungary), an authority on atmospheric physics and chemistry.

Professor *Hallan C. Noltimier* (Department of Geology & Mineralogy, Ohio State University, Columbus, OH 43210, USA), an authority on geophysics.

Professor *Arthur H. Westing* (Stockholm International Peace Research Institute, Bergshamra, S-171 73 Solna, Sweden), an authority on environmental impact of military activities.

---

[1] The symposium participants were: Professor Richard A. Falk (Princeton University), Mr Jozef Goldblat (SIPRI), Professor Anthony M. Imevbore (University of Ife, Nigeria), Professor Allan S. Krass (Hampshire College, Massachusetts), Dr Ernö Mészáros (Institute for Atmospheric Physics, Budapest), Professor Hallan C. Noltimier (Ohio State University) and Professor Arthur H. Westing (SIPRI).
  Observers at the symposium were: Mr Paolo Bifani (UNEP, Nairobi), Mr Liviu Bota (UNIDIR, Geneva), Ms Maria E. Marrassi (Unesco, Paris) and Ms Kerstin Oldfelt (UNEP, Geneva).

1. Environmental warfare: an overview

Arthur H. Westing
Stockholm International Peace Research Institute

I. Introduction

Environmental warfare refers to the manipulation of the environment for hostile military purposes. The militarily most useful hostile manipulations of the environment would be those in which a relatively modest expenditure of triggering energy leads to the release of a substantially greater amount of directed destructive energy.

Environmental warfare could, at least in principle, involve damage-causing manipulations of: (*a*) celestial bodies or space; (*b*) the atmosphere; (*c*) the land (lithosphere); (*d*) the oceans (hydrosphere); or (*e*) the biota, either terrestrial or marine (biosphere). Each of these five domains is considered in turn in the sections that follow.

A number of the hostile manipulations of today and tomorrow that comprise environmental warfare fall under the aegis of a number of disparate arms control treaties, either directly or indirectly. These legal restraints are alluded to in the concluding section. Prominent among them is the Environmental Modification (Enmod) Convention of 1977, which also receives separate treatment (see Goldblat, chapter 5; Krass, chapter 6; appendix 2). Policy recommendations are also given separate treatment (chapter 7), as is bibliographic material (appendix 1).

This analysis draws to some extent upon two earlier works by the author (Westing, 1977; 1980). Moreover, a catalogue is available elsewhere of potential hostile manipulations of the environment (Canada, 1975).

II. Celestial bodies and space

Celestial bodies refer to the Moon and other such planetary satellites, the planets themselves, the Sun and other stars, asteroids, meteors, and the like. Space refers to all of the vast region beyond our atmosphere (i.e., the region above the ionosphere) and thus, for practical purposes, begins a few hundred kilometres above the Earth's surface.

With reference to the hostile manipulation of celestial bodies, it was suggested recently that some day we might have the ability to divert asteroids, using a nuclear weapon, so as to cause them to strike enemy territory (Sullivan, 1983).

There appears to be no suggestion as yet for how space might be manipulated for hostile purposes.

III. The atmosphere

The Earth's atmosphere extends upwards some hundreds of kilometres, but becomes extraordinarily thin beyond about 150 km. It is divided into the lower atmosphere, which represents more than 99 per cent of the atmospheric mass, and the upper atmosphere, with less than 1 per cent of the mass. The lower atmosphere extends upward perhaps 55 km. It consists of the troposphere (about 0–12 km up; about 87 per cent of the total atmospheric mass) and the stratosphere (about 12–55 km). The stratosphere, in turn, can be divided into the lower stratosphere (about 12–30 km) and the upper stratosphere (about 30–55 km). The troposphere is turbulent (windy) and contains clouds whereas the stratosphere is quiescent and cloudless. The upper atmosphere (above about 55 km) consists of the mesosphere (about 55–80 km) and the ionosphere (or thermosphere) (about 80–a few hundred km). The ionized (electrified) molecules that distinguish the ionosphere serve to deflect certain radio waves downwards, thereby making possible long-distance amplitude-modulated (AM) radio communication.

Some ozone is found throughout the atmosphere, its overall average concentration being 635 μg/kg (820 μg/m^3). The atmospheric ozone is not distributed evenly, but is found largely in the lower stratosphere, indeed, largely within a so-called ozone layer (about 20–30 km up) in which the atmospheric concentration of ozone is up to 100 times the overall average. This ozone layer provides a partial barrier to solar ultraviolet radiation.

With respect to hostile manipulations of the upper atmosphere, it is sometimes suggested that techniques might be developed in the future which would make it possible to alter the electrical properties of the ionosphere in such a way as to disrupt enemy communications.[1] In fact, during the early 1960s the US Air Force carried out some short-lived experiments in which huge numbers of tiny lengths of fine copper wire were injected into the ionosphere—in this instance, however, for the opposite purpose of improving radio communications (Liller, 1964; Stevenson, 1963).

With respect to the lower atmosphere, some consider it an imminent possibility to be able to open a temporary 'window' in the ozone layer above enemy territory for the purpose of permitting an injurious level of ultraviolet radiation to penetrate to the ground, perhaps by the controlled release of a bromine

[1] High-altitude nuclear detonations would disrupt communication systems on the ground, but would do so directly by emitting an electro-magnetic pulse and not via an atmospheric manipulation (Stein, 1983).

4

compound from orbiting satellites (Sullivan, 1975). However, the direct military utility of such an action, even if it could be accomplished, would seem to be exceedingly low.

There is a report that the USA injected unknown substances into the troposphere over enemy territory during the Second Indochina War for the purpose of rendering inoperable enemy radars used for aiming defensive surface-to-air missiles (Hersh, 1972). This operation has not been acknowledged and, if it indeed occurred, there is no indication of the extent to which it succeeded.

Various levels of control over winds (e.g., creation or redirection of hurricanes), over clouds (e.g., creation or dissolution of fog, generation of cloud-to-ground lightning), or over precipitation (e.g., production of torrential rains, heavy snowfall, massive hail) could bring about direct or indirect damage to an enemy. The effective control of winds still remains beyond human capability. Control over clouds for hostile (or other) purposes remains to date at the non-existent to trivial levels (Atlas, 1977; Kerr, 1982; Mason, 1980). The one vigorously sustained attempt at rain making for hostile purposes—that by the USA during the Second Indochina War—achieved only indifferent, if any, success, technical or military (Westing, 1977, pages 55–57). A more detailed analysis of present and future capabilities regarding atmospheric manipulations is provided elsewhere (see Mészáros, chapter 2; see also Krass, chapter 6, annex 6.1).

A large-scale nuclear war would, of course, be extraordinarily disruptive to the human environment (Westing, 1981; 1982). Recent theoretical examinations of the subject have suggested that such an event would have an especially deleterious impact on the weather (Covey et al., 1984; Turco et al., 1983) and thus, in turn, on the biota (Ehrlich et al., 1983). This non-directed, collateral impact of nuclear war on the atmosphere—often referred to as the 'nuclear winter'—would, it is suggested, seriously affect an area perhaps as large as half the globe for a period of weeks or months.

IV. The lithosphere

Land covers almost 15 thousand million hectares (29 per cent) of the Earth's surface. Almost 1.6 thousand million hectares of the land (11 per cent of the total land area) is continuously ice-covered, much of this represented by Antarctica. Perhaps 1 800 million hectares (12 per cent) is desert. On another 800 million hectares (5 per cent) at least some stratum of the soil remains frozen the year round, a condition referred to as permafrost; and 200 million hectares or more (1.5 per cent) is accounted for by rugged mountain terrain. Much of the remaining 10 500 million hectares or so (71 per cent) of the land is found largely in the northern hemisphere and supports virtually the entire global population and its artefacts.

Successful manipulation of the land for hostile purposes would depend for the most part upon the ability to recognize and take advantage of local instabilities or pent-up energies, whether natural or anthropogenic. For example, some mountainous landforms are at least at certain times prone to landslides (soil and

5

rock avalanches), and some arctic or alpine sites can be prone to snow avalanches; under the right conditions either could be initiated with hostile intent. The hostile manipulation of permafrost is taken up in section VI below. A number of important rivers flow through more than one country. This situation can provide the opportunity for an upstream nation to divert the waters of such a river so as to deny their use to a downstream nation. Natural levees or constructed dikes and dams (semi-permanent anthropogenic additions to the environment) could be destroyed to release the water contained behind them; and nuclear power stations or related facilities (further cultural artefacts that have become semi-permanent features of the environment) could be damaged so as to release their radioactive contents to the surroundings. More fanciful possibilities have also been mentioned, including the instigation of earthquakes in enemy territory or the awakening of similarly located quiescent volcanoes. A more detailed analysis of present and future capabilities regarding geospheric (tectonic) manipulations is provided elsewhere (Noltimier, chapter 3).

At certain times and places, appropriate military actions can bring about highly destructive floods. The most straightforward means of accomplishing this is to breach existing levees, dikes or dams by one means or another. In a notable early instance, during the Franco-Dutch War of 1672–78, the Dutch in June 1672 were partially successful in stopping the French from overrunning the Netherlands by cutting dikes to create the so-called Holland Water Line (Baxter, 1966, pages 72–73; Blok, 1907, pages 380–381). It might be added that this manoeuvre was carried out despite the vehement objections of the local inhabitants.

The Second Sino-Japanese War of 1937–45 provides a far more devastating example of intentional military flooding (Westing, 1977, page 54). In order to curtail the Japanese advance, the Chinese in June 1938 dynamited the Huayuankow dike of the Yellow River (Huang He) near Chengchow. This action resulted in the drowning of several thousand Japanese soldiers and stopped their advance into China along this front. In the process, however, the flood waters also ravaged major portions of Henan, Anhui and Jiangsu provinces. Several million hectares of farmlands were inundated in the process, and the crops and topsoil destroyed. The river was not brought back under control until 1947. In terms of more direct human impact, the flooding inundated some 11 Chinese cities and more than 4 000 villages. At least several hundred thousand Chinese drowned as a result (and possibly many more) and several million were left homeless. Indeed, this act of environmental warfare appears to have been the most devastating single act in all human history, in terms of numbers of lives claimed.

During World War II, the British in May 1943 destroyed two major dams in the Ruhr valley, the Möhne and Eder (Brickhill, 1951, pages 95–108). There was a vast amount of damage: 125 factories were destroyed or badly damaged, 25 bridges vanished and 21 more were badly damaged, some power stations were destroyed, numerous coal mines were flooded, and railway lines were disrupted. Some 6 500 cattle and pigs were lost and 3 000 ha of arable land was ruined. The official German figure for human losses was 1 294. British Air Force authorities were enormously pleased with the results, summarized as 'maximum effect with minimum effort' (Brickhill, 1951, pages 9, 11). Also in World War II, German forces in 1944 intentionally flooded with salt water some 200 000 ha of agricultural lands in the Netherlands (Aartsen, 1946); these lands subsequently required a huge rehabilitation programme (Dorsman, 1947).

During the Korean War, US forces pursued a policy of attacking dams in North Korea (Rees, 1964, pages 381–382). The destruction of irrigation dams was considered by the USA to be among the most successful of its air operations of the Korean War (Futrell *et al.*, 1961, pages 627–628, 637).

Throughout the world there exist some 72 dams in 21 different countries that impound at least 1 thousand million cubic metres of water each, more than half of these being in either the USA or the USSR (Lane, 1984, page 137). Indeed, six of them impound more than 100 thousand million cubic metres each. These 72 major dams, as well as scores of lesser dams and various major rivers with levees or dikes, stand ever ready as potential environmental targets.

There are now about 297 nuclear-powered electrical generating stations throughout the world plus a further 15 that have been shut down (IAEA, 1983). These stations (with an average net capacity of 559 MW(e)) are found in 25 different countries. Eight countries contain at least 10 each of these enduring facilities; more than one-quarter of them are located in the USA. In addition to the 312 power stations just noted, there exist a number of spent-fuel reprocessing plants, nuclear bomb factories, nuclear-waste storage repositories, and perhaps other land-based facilities harbouring large quantities of radioactive materials.

Should any of these nuclear facilities be bombed in time of war, the possibility exists that a considerable surrounding area—measurable in terms of thousands of hectares—would become contaminated with injurious levels of strontium-90, caesium-137 and other radioactive elements (Cooper, 1978; Fetter and Tsipis, 1981; Ramberg, 1980). Such areas would defy effective decontamination and would thus remain uninhabitable for decades. It is thus fortunate that the only such nuclear station so far to have been destroyed with hostile intent (located in Iraq) had not yet begun operation at either of the two times it was attacked (Marshall, 1980; 1981).

V. The hydrosphere

The oceans of the world cover 71 per cent of the Earth's surface and border on 139 of the 169 or so nations. Indeed, some 43 of the 139 are island nations. The high seas also constitute an important military (naval) arena in their own right.

Among the hostile ocean modifications that have been suggested as military possibilities for the future are physical or chemical manipulations that are meant to disrupt acoustic (sonar) or electromagnetic properties of the attacked waters. The purpose for such attack would be the disruption of enemy underwater communication, remote sensing, navigation and missile-guidance systems. The hostile destruction of nuclear-powered ships or of supertankers and other ships carrying poisonous cargoes is discussed in section VI below.

Another possibility for environmental warfare involving the oceans is the

7

generation of tsunamis (seismic sea waves) for the purpose of destroying coastal cities and other near-shore facilities. One way that has been suggested for creating a tsunami on demand is to set off one or more nuclear devices in an appropriate underwater locality (Clark, 1961; see also Noltimier, chapter 3).

VI. The biosphere

The land supports some 4 thousand million hectares of tree-based (forest) ecosystems, about 3 thousand million hectares of grass-based (prairie) ecosystems, almost 1 thousand million hectares of lichen-based (tundra) ecosystems, and perhaps 1.5 thousand million hectares of crops (both annual and perennial). The oceans support huge expanses of algae, attached or floating, and the marine ecosystems based on them. These divers ecosystems are all expoited by humans, which could not survive without the continued harvesting of trees, livestock, fish and other renewable resources (Westing, 1980). These ecosystems additionally provide us with a series of more cryptic, though equally crucial, indirect services that keep our planet habitable (Bormann, 1976; Ehrlich and Mooney, 1983; Farnworth et al., 1981; Pimentel et al., 1980; Westman, 1977). It must therefore be noted with considerable concern that these ecosystems can be manipulated for hostile purposes in a number of ways, among them: (a) by applying chemical poisons; (b) by introducing exotic living organisms; (c) by incendiary means; and (d) by mechanical means.

Forests can be devastated for hostile purposes over huge areas by spraying them with herbicides (plant pcisons) or other means, as was demonstrated by the USA during the Second Indochina War (Westing, 1976; 1984). At certain times and places self-propagating wild fires could be initiated which would decimate large tracts of forest. For example, a temperate-zone coniferous forest might have an above-ground dry-weight biomass of 200000 kg/ha having an energy content of 15 MJ/kg, and thus 3 TJ/ha of more or less readily releasable energy. Killing the trees (i.e., the autotrophic component) of a forest ecosystem—whether by herbicides, fire or other means—can be expected to lead to substantial damage to that system's wildlife (heterotrophic component) and also to its nutrient budget, the latter via soil erosion and nutrient dumping (loss of nutrients in solution). Substantial recovery from such unbalancing of the regional ecosystem could well take decades (Westing, 1980, pages 8–10).

Prairies can be damaged for hostile purpose in the same ways that forests can (i.e., by herbicidal, incendiary or other attack). Thus during the Second Anglo-Boer War of 1899–1902 the Boers set torch to wide areas of veldt in order to deny forage to the advancing British (Wet, 1902, page 181). At an estimated above-ground dry-weight biomass of 10000 kg/ha for a prairie ecosystem, this represents a catastrophic loss to that system of perhaps 100 GJ/ha of captured and stored energy plus the loss for that growing season of food, and in some instances also cover, for the indigenous wildlife.

Tundra ecosystems can also be quite readily destroyed by one means or another, with serious ramifications (Westing, 1980, chapter 5). Under normal conditions, tundra vegetation forms an insulating layer which prevents the underlying soil from thawing too deeply during the summer and from turning into a morass. With the vegetation destroyed not only would it become virtually impossible for vehicles to traverse the area, but perhaps the potential for serious erosion would be created and the delicately balanced ecosystem would be disastrously upset for many decades.

The employment of certain biological warfare agents could, in principle, introduce exotic micro-organisms into any region on a long-term, if not permanent, basis. Such an introduction could conceivably unbalance (or adversely re-balance) the regional ecosystem to such an extent that the area became uninhabitable for an indefinite period of time. To illustrate this point in a small way, the United Kingdom used the Scottish island of Gruinard (58°N 50°W) during 1941–42 for testing the military potential of *Bacillus anthracis*, the causative agent of anthrax (Manchee *et al.*, 1981; 1983). The island remains dangerously contaminated to this day.

The several thousand oil wells drilled into the continental shelves of the world currently account for about one-fifth of world production (Westing, 1980, page 165). Well over 5 000 oil tankers ply the oceans (about one-quarter of all merchant shipping) and annually transport about half of world production over long distances. Whereas these tankers have an average capacity of $70\,000\,m^3$, perhaps three dozen of them are truly supertankers, holding more than $400\,000\,m^3$ each. Then there exist about 330 nuclear-powered ships, mostly large submarines owned by the USA or the USSR (Moore, 1984).

Marine ecosystems could be locally disrupted with hostile intent by destroying these offshore oil wells or loaded oil tankers (and other bulk carriers of poisonous cargoes) which were sailing near the shore. Recovery from such disruption (more probable as a collateral effect than a primary one) would be likely to take at least several years (Westing, 1980, pages 165–167). Similarly, the release into the near-shore marine environment of radioactive elements through the destruction of a nuclear-powered ship—while it would have little overt effect on the contaminated ecosystems itself—would preclude local human exploitation for many years (Westing, 1980, pages 160–163).

VII.   Conclusion

Control over the forces of nature for the achievement of military aims has been a human fantasy since the beginning of history. The ancient Greeks envied Zeus his ability to hurl thunderbolts. Moses was said to have been able to control the Red Sea in such a way as to drown the Egyptian forces that were pursuing the Israelites (*Exodus* 14: 27–28). Joshua claimed to have caused the Sun to stand still so that the Israelites could consummate a battle with the Anamites (*Joshua* 10: 12–13).

Those pent-up forces in the human environment that can at present be usefully released for hostile military purposes include especially: (*a*) the stored energy in the fuel represented by some forests; (*b*) the potential energy of the water held back by levees or dams; and (*c*) the decay-emitted energy of radioactive elements contained within nuclear facilities. The hostile disruption (unbalancing) of a forest, prairie or other ecosystem could also be thought of in terms of energy, that is, as the dissipation of the complex organizational energy contained within that system.

The future could conceivably bring some measure of ability to manipulate for useful hostile purposes such forces of nature as hurricanes, earthquakes or volcanoes (see Mészáros, chapter 2; Noltimier, chapter 3).

A number of international instruments enjoying varying levels of acceptance provide legal restraints against either environmental warfare *per se* or the means of waging it, whether feasible as yet or not (for the texts of these treaties, see Goldblat, 1982). Thus, the Geneva Protocol of 1925 (with 104 or more parties) prohibits the use in war of chemical or biological agents; and the Bacteriological and Toxin Weapon Convention of 1972 (with 97 or more parties) prohibits even the possession of biological or toxin agents. Protocol I of 1977 Additional to the Geneva Conventions of 1949 (with 37 or more parties) prohibits, with certain exceptions, attacks against the environment that would prejudice the health or survival of the population as well as attacks against works or installations containing dangerous forces, namely, dams, dikes and nuclear electrical generating stations (for the text of this Protocol, see appendix 3). This Protocol includes a general prohibition of the use of methods or means of warfare which are intended, or may be expected, to cause widespread, long-lasting *and* severe damage to the natural environment.[2]

The treaty most broadly applicable to environmental warfare is the Environmental Modification Convention of 1977 (with 41 or more parties) (Goldblat, chapter 5; Krass, chapter 6; appendix 2). It prohibits the hostile use of environmental modification techniques having "widespread, long-lasting *or* severe effects" as the means of damage. By environmental modification technique here is specifically meant any technique for changing—through the "deliberate manipulation" of natural processes—the dynamics, composition or structure of space or of the Earth, including its atmosphere, lithosphere, hydrosphere and biota.

As the capabilities of our planet to avoid environmental catastrophe on the one hand and military catastrophe on the other continue to diminish, one can only hope that moral, legal, common sense or other restraint will prevent techniques of environmental warfare of today or tomorrow from exacerbating our growing dilemma (see Falk, chapter 4). Thus, the nations of the world disregard at their peril the fifth general principle of the World Charter for Nature (UNGA, 1982) that, "Nature shall be secured against degradation caused by warfare or other hostile activities".

---

[2] It might be noted that the partial restrictions on the use of nuclear weapons embodied in the Outer Space Treaty of 1967 and Seabed Treaty of 1971 do not prohibit their use for possible hostile environmental modifications or other purpose in these two environmental domains.

References

Aartsen, J. P. van. 1946. Consequences of the war on agriculture in the Netherlands. *International Review of Agriculture*, Rome, **37**: 5S–34S, 49S–70S, 108S–123S.

Atlas, D. 1977. Paradox of hail suppression. *Science*, Washington, **195**: 139–145.

Baxter, S. B. 1966. *William III and the Defense of European Liberty 1650–1702*. New York: Harcourt, Brace & World, 462 pp. + 8 pl.

Blok, P. J. 1907. *History of the People of the Netherlands. IV. Frederick Henry, John deWitt, William III*. (Translated from the Dutch by O. A. Bierstadt) New York: G. P. Putnam's Sons, 566 pp. + 3 maps.

Bormann, F. H. 1976. Inseparable linkage: conservation of natural ecosystems and the conservation of fossil energy. *BioScience*, Washington, **26**: 754–760.

Brickhill, P. 1951. *Dam Busters*. London: Evans Brothers, 269 pp. + 13 pl.

Canada. 1975. *Suggested Preliminary Approach to Considering the Possibility of Concluding a Convention on the Prohibition of Environmental Modification for Military or Other Hostile Purposes*. Geneva: Conference of the Committee on Disarmament Document No. CCD/463 (5 Aug 75), 24 + 1 pp.

Clark, W. H. 1961. Chemical and thermonuclear explosives. *Bulletin of the Atomic Scientists*, Chicago, **17**: 356–360.

Cooper, C. L. 1978. Nuclear hostages. *Foreign Policy*, Washington, **1978**(32): 127–135.

Covey, C., Schneider, S. H. and Thompson, S. L. 1984. Global atmospheric effects of massive smoke injections from a nuclear war: results from general circulation model simulations. *Nature*, London, **308**: 21–25.

Dorsman, C. 1947. [Damage to horticultural crops from inundation with seawater.] (In Dutch) *Tijdschrift over Plantenziekten*, Wageningen, **53**(3): 65–86.

Ehrlich, P. R. and Mooney, H. A. 1983. Extinction, substitution, and ecosystem services. *BioScience*, Washington, **33**: 248–254.

Ehrlich, P. R. *et al.* 1983. Long-term biological consequences of nuclear war. *Science*, Washington, **222**: 1293–1300.

Farnworth, E. G., Tidrick, T. H., Jordan, C. F. and Smathers, W. M., Jr. 1981. Value of natural ecosystems: an economic and ecological framework. *Environmental Conservation*, Geneva, **8**: 275–282.

Fetter, S. A. and Tsipis, K. 1981. Catastrophic releases of radioactivity. *Scientific American*, New York, **244**(4): 33–39, 146.

Futrell, R. F., Mosely, L. S. and Simpson, A. F. 1961. *United States Air Force in Korea 1950–1953*. New York: Duell, Sloan & Pearce, 774 pp. + pl.

Goldblat, J. 1982. *Agreements for Arms Control: a Critical Survey*. London: Taylor & Francis, 387 pp. [a SIPRI book].

Hersh, S. M. 1972. Rainmaking is used as weapon by U.S. *New York Times*, 3 Jul: 1–2.

IAEA (International Atomic Energy Agency). 1983. *Nuclear Power Reactors in the World*. Vienna: International Atomic Energy Agency Reference Data Series No. 2, 48 pp.

Kerr, R. A. 1982. Cloud seeding: one success in 35 years. *Science*, Washington, **217**: 519–521.

Lane, H. U. (ed.). 1984. *World Almanac & Book of Facts*. 107th edition. New York: Newspaper Enterprise Association, 928 pp.

Liller, W. 1964. Optical effects of the 1963 Project West Ford experiment. *Science*, Washington, **143**: 437–441.

Manchee, R. J., Broster, M. G., Melling, J., Henstridge, R. M. and Stagg, A. J. 1981. *Bacillus anthracis* on Gruinard island. *Nature*, London, **294**: 254–255; **295**: 362; **296**: 598.

Manchee, R. J., Broster, M. G., Anderson, I. S., Henstridge, R. M. and Melling, J. 1983. Decontamination of *Bacillus anthracis* on Gruinard island? *Nature*, London, **303**: 239–240.

Marshall, E. 1980. Iraqi nuclear program halted by bombing. *Science*, Washington, **210**: 507–508.

Marshall, E. 1981. Fallout from the raid on Iraq. *Science*, Washington, **213**: 116–117, 120.

Mason, J. 1980. Review of three long-term cloud-seeding experiments. *Meteorological Magazine*, London, **109**: 335–344.

Moore, J. (ed.). 1984. *Jane's Fighting Ships, 1983–84*. 86th edition. London: Jane's Publishing Co., 779 pp.

Pimentel, D. *et al.* 1980. Environmental quality and natural biota. *BioScience*, Washington, **30**: 750–755.

Ramberg, B. 1980. *Destruction of Nuclear Energy Facilities in War: the Problem and the Implications*. Lexington, Mass.: Lexington Books, 195 pp.

Rees, D. 1964. *Korea: the Limited War*. New York: St. Martin's Press, 511 pp. + 15 pl.

11

Stein, D. L. 1983. Electromagnetic pulse: the uncertain certainty. *Bulletin of the Atomic Scientists*, Chicago, **39**(3): 52–56.

Stevenson, A. E. 1963. U.S. replies to Soviet charges against certain space activities. *Department of State Bulletin*, Washington, **49**: 104–107.

Sullivan, W. 1975. Ozone depletion seen as a war tool. *New York Times*, 28 Feb: 20.

Sullivan, W. 1983. Scientists ponder forcing asteroids into safe orbits. *New York Times* 4 Jan: C3, C8.

Turco, R. P., Toon, O. B., Ackerman, T. P., Pollack, J. B. and Sagan, C. 1983. Nuclear winter: global consequences of multiple nuclear explosions. *Science*, Washington, **222**: 1283–1292.

UNGA (United Nations General Assembly). 1982. *World Charter for Nature*. New York: UN General Assembly Resolution No. 37/7 (28 Nov 82), 5 pp.

Westing, A. H. 1976. In: SIPRI (eds). *Ecological Consequences of the Second Indochina War*. Stockholm: Almqvist & Wiksell, 119 pp. + 8 pl.

Westing, A. H. 1977. Geophysical and environmental weapons. In: SIPRI. *Weapons of Mass Destruction and the Environment*. London: Taylor & Francis, 95 pp.: chap. 3 (pp. 49–63).

Westing, A. H. 1980. In: SIPRI (eds). *Warfare in a Fragile World: Military Impact on the Human Environment*. London: Taylor & Francis, 249 pp.

Westing, A. H. 1981. Environmental impact of nuclear warfare. *Environmental Conservation*, Geneva, **8**: 269–273.

Westing, A. H. 1982. Environmental consequences of nuclear warfare. *Environmental Conservation*, Geneva, **9**: 269–272.

Westing, A. H. (ed.). 1984. *Herbicides in War: the Long-term Ecological and Human Consequences*. London: Taylor & Francis, 210 pp. [a SIPRI book].

Westman, W. E. 1977. How much are nature's services worth? *Science*, Washington, **197**: 960–964.

Wet, C. R. de. 1902. *Three Years War (October 1899–June 1902)*. (Translated from the Dutch) Westminster, England: Archibald Constable, 520 pp. + 1 map.

2. Techniques for manipulating the atmosphere

Ernö Mészáros

Institute for Atmospheric Physics, Budapest

I. Introduction

Weather and climate influence human life in many ways. Variations in the state of the atmosphere in the short term—that is, of the weather—modify agricultural production and transportation and influence human behaviour. Variations in the long-term climate can even determine the fate of a given civilization.

For these reasons, humans have always attempted to understand, predict and even modify atmospheric phenomena. Despite these efforts, insufficient knowledge, lack of adequate instrumentation and the sheer complexity of the problem have permitted scientific meteorology to develop only during the past century. Even now our knowledge of the atmosphere is far from sufficient. It is clear, however, that we have now attained the technical sophistication to attempt the modification of certain weather phenomena, especially those related to clouds and precipitation: for example, rain stimulation, cloud and fog dissipation and hail suppression. Moreover, human activity is beginning to modify the weather inadvertently, for example, by altering the land surface and by releasing heat and materials into the atmosphere.

It is unfortunate that, parallel with the growth in our knowledge of the atmosphere and our ability to modify it, military circles have begun to consider the possibility of manipulating the weather for hostile purposes. Indeed, 'meteorological' weapons were already used during the Second Indochina War, where the USA attempted to augment rainfall in order to render enemy trails impassable (Westing, 1977, pages 55–57). Moreover, recent model calculations suggest that the fearful threat of large-scale nuclear war to the human environment extends to significant disturbance of the atmosphere (Covey *et al.*, 1984; Izrael, 1983; Turco *et al.*, 1983). From this follows that longer-term changes in our environment might be as terrible as the immediate consequences (Ehrlich *et al.*, 1983).

This chapter summarizes the state of the art regarding the possibilities and techniques for intentionally modifying the lower atmosphere (about 0–55 km in

13

height and containing more than 99 per cent of the total atmospheric mass): that is, the troposphere (about 0–12 km) plus the stratosphere (about 12–55 km). As will be noted, the various modifications to be described all appear to possess at least some level of potential hostile military application.

II. Modification of the Earth's surface

Weather and climate are in part dependent upon the character of the Earth's surface. The atmosphere–geosphere system of concern in this regard consists of: (a) the atmosphere; (b) the lithosphere (continental land surfaces); (c) the biosphere (the terrestrial vegetation being of particular interest); and (d) the hydrosphere (oceans). The extent of continental and oceanic ice cover is also of great importance in regulating this system. Of the radiant solar energy reaching the atmosphere–geosphere system (i.e., the incident solar energy), about one-third is reflected back into space, primarily by the atmosphere (mostly by the clouds) and secondarily by the Earth's surface. The fraction of the incident solar energy reflected back from the system is referred to as the 'planetary albedo', which is comprised of 'atmospheric albedo' and 'surface albedo'. Another third of the incident radiant solar energy is absorbed by the atmosphere; and the final third is absorbed by the Earth's surface (i.e., by the lithosphere, biosphere and hydrosphere).

The radiant energy absorbed by the Earth's surface heats the surface and also serves to evaporate water. A part is re-radiated into the atmosphere in the form of thermal energy, heating the lower atmosphere. The regional radiation balance (the relationship between incoming and outgoing energy) determines the temperature in that region, whereas the differences in radiation balance from one region to another (e.g., between the equator and the poles) constitute the driving force for the circulation of the atmosphere (the wind systems). It is thus clear that the energy reflection, retention and re-radiation characteristics of the geosphere have a substantial influence on weather and climate. It is equally obvious that surface albedo is strongly dependent upon the nature of the surface. For example, dicotyledonous (broadleafed) forest in summer has an albedo of about 0.18 (i.e., reflects back into space 18 per cent of the incident radiant energy); either coniferous forest or tundra in summer, 0.13; a forest in winter with stable snow, 0.45; arctic snow, 0.80; and the oceans, 0.07 to 0.23 (Wilson et al., 1971, page 157). Any change in surface properties alters the radiation balance and thus the heating of the troposphere and thereby weather patterns.

Polar ice

The most sensitive part of the Earth's surface from the point of view of climatic variation is the polar ice cover, the areal extent of which varies remarkably in a time frame of hundreds of millions of years, but changes little in a time frame of centuries. However, the present ice cover is considered to be in a state of unstable equilibrium, that is, if the ice were to disappear it would reform in only a limited way (Mercer, 1978; see also Noltimier, chapter 3). Such an event would raise the sea level substantially and have a dramatic (though less readily quantifiable) effect on global climate. Just the melting of the East Antarctic ice sheet would, it has been calculated, raise the sea level on a world-wide basis by about 70 m (Kukla and Gavin, 1981).

It is thought that anthropogenic increases in atmospheric carbon dioxide over the past century or so have resulted in a warmer atmosphere (owing to the so-called greenhouse effect) and thereby in a modest shrinking of the polar ice sheets that in turn has led to a rise in the world-wide sea level of perhaps 20 cm (Kukla and Gavin, 1981; Mercer, 1978; Wilson et al., 1971). A more recent factor contributing to the observed atmospheric warming appears to have been anthropogenic increases in the atmosphere of ultra-fine solid and liquid particles—so-called aerosols—which strongly absorb solar radiation. Such aerosols, containing both sulphur compounds and soot, have been newly described for the Arctic region (Rahn, 1981; Rosen et al., 1981). Moreover, the soot becomes deposited on the snow, reducing its albedo and increasing the amount that melts (Chýlek et al., 1983).

If the arctic soot load were significantly increased—whether inadvertently, incidentally or intentionally—this would pose a threat to the stability of our present global climate. Moreover, modification of the ice sheet in Antarctica could occur through either natural processes (e.g., climatic changes) or human action. It has been suggested that a nuclear explosion at a site of great instability, such as the Byrd glacier, would decouple the West Antarctic ice sheet with dramatic effects on the world-wide sea level and climate (Noltimier, chapter 3).

The oceans

It may be technically possible in the future to mechanically mix the top 150 m or so of local ocean areas (Wilson et al., 1971, pages 162–163). Such manipulation would decrease the surface temperature somewhat during the summer and increase it during the winter. Moreover, if ocean water were used for cooling purposes in a large electrical generating station, the discharge waters would locally warm surface temperatures, and surface-active materials (surfactants) could be locally applied to the ocean surface, thereby providing a barrier to evaporation and heat flow.

Such local ocean manipulations would have an effect on regional weather patterns, but the nature and extent of the effect are obscure. Numerical modelling could shed some light on the matter and might suggest the level of utility of such manipulations for either peaceful or hostile purposes.

Land surface

Use of the land for agriculture provides one of the most ancient examples of anthropogenic modification of the land surface that has had a substantial effect on climate. Some 10 per cent of the global land surface has been converted to agriculture (Westing, 1980, page 22), and altogether perhaps as much as 20 per cent has been drastically altered (Wilson *et al.*, 1971, page 12). The accompanying changes in albedo, in soil bacteria (which generate atmospheric gases such as carbon dioxide) and in heat balance (especially where irrigation is practised and in urban and industrial areas) all have a significant influence on weather and climate. However, the possibility of making deliberate changes of the land surface for the purpose of altering weather or climate—whether for civil or military purposes—appears to be remote.

One manipulation of the land surface that could have an adverse effect on the weather is the instigation of rural (forest or grassland) and urban/industrial wild fires since these would generate large amounts of smoke, that is, soot and other aerosols. It has been suggested with some authority that a large-scale nuclear war would initiate such fires on a huge enough scale to have a dramatic hemispheric impact on the weather for a period of weeks or months (Crutzen and Birks, 1982; Turco *et al.*, 1983).

III. Modification of the troposphere

The atmosphere is a mixture of different gases and aerosols, both solid and liquid. The meteorological role of the atmospheric constituents is very important since they control the radiation transfer through the atmosphere (Mészáros, 1981, chapter 6). In this way they make a substantial contribution to the control of weather and climate. Thus, any modification in the composition of the atmosphere can be followed by changes in weather patterns. Manipulations of the troposphere will be discussed under three headings: (*a*) the gaseous composition; (*b*) the aerosol concentration; and (*c*) clouds.

The gaseous composition

In considering manipulations of the troposphere at least two parameters must be taken into consideration: (*a*) the concentration of the constituent in question; and (*b*) its residence time (i.e., the average time spent in the atmosphere by its molecules).

Concentration is an important consideration with respect to manipulations of the troposphere because only concentrations of less than perhaps $1 \, mL/m^3$ could be altered to any meaningful degree (table 2.1). By way of example, carbon dioxide has a concentration of about 300 times this value. There has been an ever-increasing introduction of this substance into the atmosphere for the past 130 years (largely through the burning of fossil fuels), the current anthropogenic additions exceeding 26×10^{12} kg/year (Westing, 1980, pages 77–78), of which roughly half remains in the atmosphere. However, this long-sustained massive introduction of carbon dioxide into the atmosphere has to date increased its concentration by only about 14 per cent.

Residence time is an important consideration with respect to manipulations of the troposphere because it is a major determinant of the extent or scale of transport (table 2.1). Manipulations of a constituent with a residence time of less

Table 2.1. Gaseous composition of the unpolluted troposphere: major constituents plus selected trace constituents.

Gas	Concentration (per m³)	Total (kg)	Residence time[a]	Transport scale[b]
Nitrogen (N_2)	781 L	3.86×10^{18}	c. 10^6 years	Global
Oxygen (O_2)	209 L	1.18×10^{18}	5 000 years	Global
Argon (Ar)	9.34 L	65.8×10^{15}		
Water vapor (H_2O)[c]	0.04–40 L	c. 14×10^{15}	10 d	Regional
Carbon dioxide (CO_2)[d]	c. 330 mL	c. 2.57×10^{15}	5–6 years	Global
Nitrous oxide (N_2O)	250–350 μL	$2.0–2.7 \times 10^{12}$	c. 25 years	Global
Ozone (O_3)[e]	10–50 μL	$85–420 \times 10^9$	c. 2 years	Global
Sulphur dioxide (SO_2)	0.03–30 μL	$0.35–350 \times 10^9$	c. 2 d	Regional
Nitrogen dioxide (NO_2)	0.1–5 μL	$0.57–29 \times 10^9$	8–10 d	Regional
Others[f]	several mL	several 10^9		
Total	**1 000 L**	**c. 5.1×10^{18}**		

[a] The residence time of a gas refers to the average time spent in the atmosphere by its molecules.

[b] The transport scale of a gas is regional if the residence time is less than 1 month; it is hemispheric if the residence time is longer than about 1 month, but less than 1 year; and it is global if the residence time is longer than about 1 year.

[c] The concentration of water vapour in the troposphere is highly variable, but has an average world-wide concentration of perhaps 6 L/m³.

[d] The concentration of carbon dioxide in the troposphere has increased from a value of about 290 mL/m³ in 1850 to a value at present of about 330 mL/m³, this increase having been the result of inadvertent anthropogenic additions (largely through the burning of fossil fuels).

[e] The concentration of ozone is up to 100 times greater in the stratosphere than in the troposphere so that the average overall atmospheric concentration is about 385 μL/m³.

[f] Other trace gases include Ne, He, Kr, Xe, H_2, CH_4, CH_3Cl, Rn, CO, NH_3 and H_2S.

Source: Adapted from Mészáros (1981, page 12); total amounts calculated from data in the *Handbook of Chemistry and Physics 1979–1980*.

than a month would create a regional effect; for a constituent with a residence time of more than about a month but less than a year, manipulation would create a hemispheric effect; and for a constituent with a residence time of more than about a year, the effect would be global. A manipulation that leads to a regional effect could have potential military utility. One possible candidate for hostile purposes might be sulphur dioxide, a trace constituent with brief residence time.

Sulphur dioxide is emitted into the atmosphere mostly by the burning of sulphur-containing fossil fuels. It becomes a major constituent of so-called acid rain, an air pollutant of growing concern, especially in the developed nations. Acid rain can cause serious damage to both terrestrial (including agricultural) and freshwater ecosystems. The trans-boundary transport of sulphur dioxide is already causing international tensions in both Europe and North America. It is conceivable that a suitably situated state could covertly introduce sulphur dioxide into the atmosphere so as to debilitate the economy of a neighbouring downwind state.

Nuclear weapons detonated in the troposphere produce huge amounts of nitrogen oxides, doing so through high-temperature-mediated reactions between the nitrogen and oxygen of the atmosphere (Crutzen and Birks, 1982). In the event of a large-scale nuclear war these nitrogen oxides would contribute to the formation of so-called smog and thereby exacerbate the smoke pollution that would be generated by the many forest, grassland, urban and industrial wild fires which are sure to be initiated. The nitrogen oxides would also result in the enhancement of acid rain fall.

The aerosol concentration

Suspended within the lower atmosphere are many tiny solid and liquid particles (Mészáros, 1981, chapter 4). These particles are referred to as coarse aerosols if their diameter exceeds 1 μm, and as fine aerosols if their diameter is less than 1 μm. The aerosols dispersed from the land surface are usually coarse and contain such soil elements as aluminium, silicon, calcium or iron. Those originating from the oceans are coarse and consist mostly of sodium and chlorine. Those produced by the condensation of atmospheric gases are fine and generally contain sulphur, nitrogen or carbon. The total number of aerosol particles falls between $100 \times 10^6/m^3$ in clean air and $100 \times 10^9/m^3$ in polluted air (e.g., over urban centres). They have a combined mass of $1-100\,\mu g/m^3$. Inadvertent anthropogenic emissions of fine aerosol have been estimated to come to 300 Tg/year globally (Jaenicke, 1981) and thus (considering the ice-free land surface) to an annual production of about 2 300 kg/km².

Aerosols play an important role in the control of atmospheric optics, radiation transfer, temperature, vertical stability of the air and cloud formation (Jaenicke, 1981; Kellogg, 1980). The residence time of aerosol particles (whether of natural or of anthropogenic origin) is of the order of a week and their influence is thus felt on a regional scale.

Gray et al. (1976) have speculated that it would require an injection into the troposphere (over a period of some hours) of about 25 kg/km² of carbon particles with a diameter of 0.1 μm to absorb 15 per cent of the incident solar radiation, and presumably thereby create a substantial environmental effect for a period of several days. They suggest how such a manipulation might be accomplished on a regional basis by burning a liquid high-molecular-weight hydrocarbon in the afterburner of jet engines, but apparently no such trial has been carried out by these individuals or others.

A large-scale nuclear war would introduce huge amounts of soil and soot aerosols into the atmosphere, altogether perhaps as much at one time as the present total annual anthropogenic introductions (Crutzen and Birks, 1982). As suggested earlier, these introductions would be certain to have dramatic effects on hemispheric weather conditions for a period of weeks or months (Covey et al., 1984; Turco et al., 1983).

Clouds

The formation of clouds and the subsequent release of rainfall are complex processes, the details of which, however, have now been fairly well elucidated (Mason, 1971). In simple terms, the formation of clouds is related to the cooling of the air. The cooling is generally caused by upward translocation of an air mass. The colder the temperature, the less is the water content that can remain in vapour form. At a certain point the air becomes saturated with water vapour and condensation begins. The water vapour condenses on aerosol particles (the so-called condensation nuclei), freezing in the process. As the temperature drops below $0°C$, the major part of the water remains in a liquid (so-called super-cooled) state until about $-40°C$. Once sufficiently large, the ice crystals that form begin to fall, melt and coalesce to become rainfall.

Rainfall enhancement

Early attempts to stimulate rainfall date back to the mid-1940s. Since that time many trials have been carried out owing to the great potential importance of such weather modification for the enhancement of agricultural and other human pursuits. A closely related endeavour has been the attempt to manipulate hail-producing clouds in order to reduce hail damage.

Clouds are manipulated in a number of ways in the attempt to stimulate rainfall. Clouds have been seeded with artificial ice-initiating substances to form crystals or with coarse hygroscopic (water-absorbing) nuclei to form large droplets. A much-employed seeding agent of the former type is silver iodide; other such agents include lead iodide and copper sulphide. Under field conditions silver iodide produces about 50×10^{15} particles per kilogram. An aircraft-mounted generator dispenses the seeding agent at a rate of 0.5–1 kg/h.

Large-scale field trials of rainfall enhancement have in a number of instances increased rainfall by 10–20 per cent. In these trials, winter stratiform clouds in Tasmania, orographic clouds in central USA and winter continental cumulus clouds in Israel were found to be more amenable to rainfall enhancement than maritime and summer continental cumulus clouds in Australia or the USA. It was also found that to be amenable to rainfall enhancement a cloud had to have a temperature colder than $-10°C$. The seeding of warm clouds has been attempted in a number of ways (e.g., with sodium chloride), but so far without success.

The one attempt to date at enhancing rainfall for hostile purposes, that by the USA during the Second Indochina War, did not prove to be successful (Westing, 1977, pages 55–57), presumably because the clouds were of the wrong sort.

Rainfall deprivation

An interesting and important question related to the manipulation of clouds is whether rainfall enhancement in one locality would deprive another, downwind locality of rainfall. There has been no demonstration of such redistribution to date, although there are perhaps some indications that it might occur. A manipulation of this sort, if it were possible, could be conceived to have potential for hostile use.

Hurricane manipulation

There are some theoretical and experimental reasons to suggest that the seeding of tropical cumulus clouds using massive amounts of artificial ice nuclei such as silver iodide (or perhaps with cement powder), including hurricane-associated ones, might modify the dynamics of the hurricane system (Simpson and Dennis, 1973). However, in spite of some attempts, the manipulation of hurricanes is still very much in its infancy.

Fog dissipation

There has been some success with the dissipation of super-cooled fogs—for example, over airports—by seeding them with artificial ice nuclei (Gaivoronski *et al.*, 1967). However, the dissipation of warm fogs has not proved possible.

Lightning manipulation

The generation and separation of electric charges in thunder clouds are closely linked with the formation of rainfall (Mason, 1971, chapter 9). However, the seeding of thunder clouds has neither increased nor decreased the number or intensity of lightning discharges.

Hail manipulation

The formation of hail in thunder clouds is a very complex process. Nevertheless, some field trials have suggested that if artificial ice nuclei are introduced into suitable portions of a cloud (as determined by radar observation) the formation of hail can be suppressed (Fedorov, 1975). On the other hand, in some such trials seeding appears to have produced the opposite effect, that is, of promoting the formation of hail (Atlas, 1977). This implies the possibility that in the future reliable techniques might be developed to increase the number or intensity of crop-damaging hail storms in some region for hostile purposes.

IV. Modification of the stratosphere

Mixing between the turbulent (windy) troposphere and non-turbulent stratosphere is generally slow. As a result, the residence time of the stratospheric constituents is largely controlled by chemical processes. Moreover, since the concentration of air molecules in the stratosphere is much lower than in the troposphere, the stratospheric domain is much more sensitive to the injection of any materials. Discussed here are the stratospheric ozone layer and the stratospheric aerosol layer.

The ozone layer

Some ozone (O_3) is distributed throughout the atmosphere (table 2.1), but it is found in relatively high concentration in only the lower stratosphere, in a so-called ozone layer situated at roughly 20–30 km above the Earth's surface. The ozone layer is important to life on Earth because it provides a partial barrier to dangerous solar ultraviolet radiation.

The ozone layer forms naturally as a result of photochemical (ultraviolet-mediated) dissociation of the O_2 oxygen molecule. An equilibrium is maintained inasmuch as the ozone in turn breaks down naturally by reacting with nitrous oxide or methyl chloride (much of the former originating with soil micro-organisms and much of the latter from the oceans) and in other ways. Various human actions contribute to a possible diminution of the ozone layer, among them introductions of nitrogen oxides originating with fertilizers or with emissions from high-flying supersonic aircraft, and of halocarbons ('freons') that had been used as refrigerants, solvents or propellants. It can be calculated that a doubling of the nitrous oxide concentration in the atmosphere might lead to a decrease in the ozone concentration of about 10 per cent.

In principle it is conceivable that a 'window' could be opened in the ozone layer over an enemy's territory by emitting into the lower stratosphere halogen (e.g., bromine or chlorine) or nitrogen oxide compounds from satellites (Westing, chapter 1, section III). However, stratospheric dynamics (including a zonal mixing rate of several weeks) would make this a most difficult task.

A large-scale nuclear war would, as noted above, generate huge amounts of nitrogen oxides. The portion of these nitrogen oxides that find their way to the lower stratosphere will degrade the ozone layer to a substantial extent for a period of perhaps several years, and this would presumably have serious biological consequences (Westing, 1982).

The aerosol layer

It has been known for some two decades that an aerosol layer exists in the stratosphere, at a height of approximately 15–25 km (Jaenicke, 1981; Kellogg, 1980). This layer, which is composed mostly of sulphate particles, originates primarily from gaseous emissions of volcanoes. It exerts a strong influence on the transfer of radiation through the stratosphere and thereby on climate as well. Indeed, it has recently been suggested that volcanic activity is one of the most important factors controlling climatic fluctuations (Toon and Pollack, 1982).

It has been proposed that the stratospheric aerosol layer could be augmented in order to counteract the tropospheric warming being caused by the anthropogenic increases in carbon dioxide (Budyko, 1974). This would be done by continually introducing sulphur dioxide into the lower stratosphere from aircraft regularly flying in this domain. Carrying out similar actions for hostile purposes seems improbable.

Elsewhere in this book it is suggested that volcanoes could conceivably be stimulated to erupt for hostile purposes (Noltimier, chapter 3); on the basis of what was noted above, such action would have the collateral effect of influencing the climate. A large-scale nuclear war would also inject substantial amounts of solid aerosol into the stratosphere with similar consequences.

V. Conclusion

It follows from the foregoing presentation that a number of techniques are already available to modify the atmosphere for hostile purposes. Thus, it appears possible to enhance the rainfall from certain clouds by 10–20 per cent. Transportation could thereby be made more difficult in enemy territory or damaging floods could be intensified. Super-cooled fogs could be dissipated to reveal targets. Under certain conditions, it is possible to intensify air-pollution episodes over enemy territory by intentionally generating acid-raid or smog-producing substances. Acts of this sort could perhaps even be carried out covertly in times of peace to debilitate another nation's terrestrial and freshwater ecosystems.

Future possibilities for the hostile manipulation of the atmosphere include the modification of clouds to bring about damage-causing hail storms or lightning discharges in enemy territory. The dynamics and direction of hurricanes might in time be alterable for hostile purposes, and it may become possible to reduce the stratospheric ozone layer over enemy territory, thereby permitting undesirable levels of ultraviolet radiation to reach the ground.

Finally it must be emphasized that a large-scale nuclear war is certain to have a catastrophic collateral impact on the atmosphere and thus on weather and climate.

References

Atlas, D. 1977. Paradox of hail suppression. *Science*, Washington, **195**: 139–145.

Budyko, M. I. 1974. [*Climate and Modification of the Stratospheric Aerosol Layer.*] (In Russian) Moscow: Gidrometeoizdat, 42 pp.

Chýlek, P., Ramaswamy, V. and Srivastava, V. 1983. Albedo of soot-contaminated snow. *Journal of Geophysical Research*, Washington, **88**: 10837–10843.

Covey, C., Schneider, S. H. and Thompson, S. L. 1984. Global atmospheric effects of massive smoke injections from a nuclear war: results from general circulation model simulations. *Nature*, London, **308**: 21–25.

Crutzen, P. J. and Birks, J. W. 1982. Atmosphere after a nuclear war: twilight at noon. *Ambio*, Stockholm, **11**: 114–125.

Ehrlich, P. R. *et al.* 1983. Long-term biological consequences of nuclear war. *Science*, Washington, **222**: 1293–1300.

Fedorov, E. K. 1975. Disarmament in the field of geophysical weapons. *Scientific World*, London, **19**(3–4): 49–54.

Gaivoronski, I. I., Krasnovskaia, L. I., Miroshnichenko, V. I. and Seregin, Y. A. 1967. [Some problems in the modification of super-cooled fogs in surface air.] (In Russian) In: Gaivoronski, I. I. and Nikandrov, V. Y. (eds). [*Studies on Cloud Physics and Weather Modification.*] Moscow: Gidrometeoizdat, 274 pp.: pp. 218–226.

Gray, W. M., Frank, W. M., Corrin, M. L. and Stokes, C. A. 1976. Weather modification by carbon dust absorption of solar energy. *Journal of Applied Meteorology*, Boston, **15**: 355–386.

Izrael, Y. A. 1983. [Ecological consequences of possible nuclear war.] (In Russian) *Meteorologiya i Gidrologiya*, Moscow, **10**: 5–10.

Jaenicke, R. 1981. Atmospheric aerosols and global climate. In: Berger, A. (ed.). *Climatic Variations and Variability: Facts and Theories*. Dordrecht, Netherlands: D. Reidel, 795 pp.: pp. 577–597.

Kellogg, W. W. 1980. Aerosols and climate. In: Bach, W., Pankrath, J. and Williams, J. (eds). *Interactions of Energy and Climate*. Dordrecht, Netherlands: D. Reidel, 569 pp.: pp. 281–296.

Kukla, G. and Gavin, J. 1981. Summer ice and carbon dioxide. *Science*, Washington, **214**: 497–503.

Mason, B. J. 1971. *Physics of Clouds*. 2nd ed. Oxford: Clarendon Press, 671 pp. + 36 pl.

Mercer, J. H. 1978. West Antarctic ice sheet and CO_2 greenhouse effect: a threat of disaster. *Nature*, London, **271**: 321-325.

Mészáros, E. 1981. *Atmospheric Chemistry: Fundamental Aspects*. Amsterdam: Elsevier Scientific Publishing Co., 201 pp. [Also: Budapest: Akadémiai Kiadó.]

Rahn, K. A. 1981. Relative importances of North America and Eurasia as sources of arctic aerosol. *Atmospheric Environment*, Oxford, **15**: 1447-1455.

Rosen, H., Novakov, T. and Bodhaine, B. A. 1981. Soot in the arctic. *Atmospheric Environment*, Oxford, **15**: 1371-1374.

Simpson, J. and Dennis, A. S. 1974. Cumulus clouds and their modification. In: Hess, W. N. (ed.). *Weather and Climate Modification*. New York: John Wiley, 842 pp.: pp. 229-281.

Toon, O. B. and Pollack, J. B. 1982. Stratospheric aerosols and climate. In: Whitten, R. C. (ed.). *Stratospheric Aerosol Layer*. West Berlin: Springer Verlag, 152 pp.: pp. 121-147.

Turco, R. P., Toon, O. B., Ackerman, T. P., Pollack, J. B. and Sagan, C. 1983. Nuclear winter: global consequences of multiple nuclear explosions. *Science*, Washington, **222**: 1283-1292.

Westing, A. H. 1977. Geophysical and environmental weapons. In: SIPRI (eds). *Weapons of Mass Destruction and the Environment*. London: Taylor & Francis, 95 pp.: chap. 3 (pp. 49-63).

Westing, A. H. 1980. In: SIPRI (eds). *Warfare in a Fragile World: Military Impact on the Human Environment*. London: Taylor & Francis, 249 pp.

Westing, A. H. 1982. Environmental consequences of nuclear warfare. *Environmental Conservation*, Geneva, **9**: 269-272.

Wilson, C. L. *et al*. 1971. *Inadvertent Climate Modification: Report of the Study of Man's Impact on Climate (SMIC)*. Cambridge, Mass.: MIT Press, 308 pp.

3. Techniques for manipulating the geosphere[1]

Hallan C. Noltimier
Ohio State University

I. Introduction

Major changes to parts of the Earth's surface and pollution of the atmosphere, especially since the industrial revolution, have resulted from relentless efforts to modify the natural environment for agricultural and economic purposes. In the normal proclivity of humankind to disregard the impact upon the environment we have been methodically engaged in global war upon ourselves, unwitting though this may be.

This study concerns not such incidental environmental disruption, but rather the ability to disrupt the geosphere (lithosphere plus hydrosphere) for hostile purposes, so-called geophysical warfare. The goal of such attack upon the terrestrial or marine environment might be the disruption of a target country's economy, standard of living, ability to wage war or even future survival. Hostile acts on this scale, however, might also threaten the quality of the environment of other countries not involved in the dispute or even of the perpetrator. It will be shown here that certain substantial modifications of the geosphere are technically possible and that they could have grave environmental ramifications.

II. Geophysical warfare

The efficient pursuit of hostile manipulations of the geosphere is characterized by the employment of a modest amount of precisely placed energy which, in turn, triggers the release of vastly more energy (MacDonald, 1968). The problem is to estimate correctly the consequences of this induced energy release, an energy release over which neither the victim nor the perpetrator has any real means of control.

Among the hostile manipulations of the geosphere to be considered here at

---

[1] This chapter was adapted by the editor from the author's more detailed SIPRI/UNIDIR symposium presentation.

least briefly are: (*a*) triggering earthquakes; (*b*) generating tsunamis (seismic sea waves); (*c*) triggering landslides; (*d*) fluidizing thixotropic soils (so-called quick clays); (*e*) activating quiescent volcanoes; (*f*) breaching water containments; (*g*) melting polar ice; and (*h*) disrupting permafrost soils. Most of these potential manipulations are characterized by geomorphic instabilities capable of releasing large, or even vast, amounts of potential energy with destructive effect. However, the instabilities differ greatly in their susceptibility to be triggered and in their ability to be spatially controlled or directed (aimed).

Triggering of earthquakes

Earthquakes can, of course, result in spectacular damage to the environment. The question thus arises in any consideration of hostile manipulations of the lithosphere whether earthquakes could in some way be triggered in enemy territory.

It has been established through the detailed analysis of seismic activity at nuclear-weapon test sites that underground nuclear explosions of even modest size in tectonically stable areas lead to a transitory increase in the numbers of discernible earth tremors (Boucher *et al.*, 1969; Emiliani *et al.*, 1969; see also Bolt, 1976). It is important to note, however, that all of the aftershocks that could be attributed to the underground nuclear detonations had magnitudes that were at least an order of magnitude (i.e., a factor of 10) less severe than the triggering blast had been. The typical range of loss in the translation from nuclear energy to seismic energy appears to be between two and three orders of magnitude (i.e., between a hundred-fold and a thousand-fold loss) (Bolt, 1976, page 39).

Natural earthquakes occur in association with tectonically unstable areas, for example, along the San Andreas fault zone in California. Along such fault lines the frequency and severity of earthquakes seem to be controlled by so-called sticking points (asperities). It has recently been reported that the locations of such sticking points can be identified more or less readily and with a greater or lesser degree of confidence (see, e.g., Kerr, 1983; 1984). Perhaps the action of a nuclear explosion could release a sticking point, although tectonic evidence (regarding the typical depth of an earthquake focus and so forth) suggests that the detonation would probably have to occur at a depth of 5 km or more. It is thus most improbable that an earthquake could be triggered for hostile purposes in enemy territory.

Generation of tsunamis

Tsunamis (sea waves) are the result of seismic activity on a continental shelf. Underwater earthquakes are associated with fault zones on the shelf and these could lead to the slumping that generates a destructive tsunami. It is thus of interest to note that recent geophysical studies of the continental shelf of the western north Atlantic have revealed the prevalence of hitherto unrecognized fault zones, for example, off the coast of New Jersey (Noltimier, 1974; Prior *et al.*, 1984). Moreover, it has just been discovered that a massive slab of the southwestern Norwegian coast (having a volume of more than $10^{12}\,m^3$) slid towards the vicinity of the Shetland Islands during the recent geological past, suggesting geological instability on that side of the Atlantic as well (Lange, 1983).

An underwater nuclear explosion (or co-ordinated series of explosions) at the continental shelf/slope margin might cause a slumping that would generate a tsunami (Clark, 1961). For example, if advantage were taken of the instabilities off the New Jersey coast, massive damage would occur to the industrial and port facilities of the greater New York city area.

Triggering of landslides

In mountainous terrain, earthquakes can set off landslides—that is, soil and rock avalanches—that cause high death tolls and much environmental damage. Such landslides can be treacherous events since they might involve a million cubic metres ($3 \times 10^9\,kg$) or more of soil and rock, moving down-slope at velocities in excess of $3\,m/s$ for distances of several or more kilometres. At least two dozen events of such magnitude, usually triggered by earthquakes of Richter magnitudes between about 7 and 9, are known to have occurred in recent decades (Keefer, 1984). In one spectacular instance in October 1963 some 240 million cubic metres of soil and rock slid into the Vaiont reservoir in north-eastern Italy, having been triggered by heavy rains. This mass movement caused the stored water to spill over the dam, sweeping away a number of villages and drowning some 2 500 people in a matter of moments. Whereas the Vaiont dam, the highest thin-arch dam in the world, was a marvel of engineering, the choice of site in this geologically unstable environment was a marvel of incompetence. Perhaps the most destructive rock avalanche during this century occurred at Nevados Huascarán, Peru in May 1970 and is said to have killed some 18 000 persons. It had been triggered by an earthquake of Richter magnitude 7.9.

A properly aimed nuclear bomb of 100 kT or more would appear to suffice to trigger a massive rock avalanche in a geologically unstable mountainous area.

Fluidization of thixotropic soils

Certain seemingly ordinary clay soils possess the peculiar ability to become fluid while being subjected to even modest seismic vibrations. These thixotropic soils (or 'quick clays') are marine clays comprised of glacial rock flour rich in sodium chloride or other electrolyte. Such soils are most prevalent in northern latitudes throughout the world, although they are not confined to such locations.

Severe environmental damage can result from the transitory fluidization (liquefaction) of thixotropic soils. For example, the March 1964 Alaska earthquake had its epicentre some 130 km east of Anchorage, yet resulted in serious damage to that city because it is situated on soil of this sort (Griggs and Gilchrist, 1983, pages 121–123; Oakeshott, 1976, pages 7–9). The clay simply liquified in response to the seismic vibrations and flowed down-slope into the harbour, taking much of the city with it. Following the brief earthquake the clay again became as firm as before.

It is speculated that in potentially unstable terrain of this sort a surface or sub-surface burst of perhaps a 100 kT nuclear bomb would generate soil vibrations that would result in considerable regional damage to the environment. Moreover, the location of thixotropic soils can be identified from aerial photography (Griggs and Gilchrist, 1983, page 123).

Activation of quiescent volcanoes

World-wide, there are perhaps 750 volcanoes classified as being active, some 75 per cent of them comprising the so-called ring of fire that circumscribes the Pacific Ocean basin; others are within the Mediterranean region, along the mid-Atlantic ridge in Antarctica, the Kamchatka peninsula and elsewhere (Fedotov and Markhinin, 1983; Oakeshott, 1976). Such active (geologically unstable) volcanoes are quiescent most of the time, but erupt occasionally at essentially un-predictable times. A number of them pose a threat to urban and industrial areas and to various large dams; and a few have the potential to alter the weather on a hemispheric, if not global, scale. Volcanic eruptions cause environmental damage through the flow of lava, by depositing ash, mud or rock, by introducing fine particulate matter (dust) and harmful gases into the atmosphere, and in other ways. (For an examination of the effects of extraneous introductions into the atmosphere, see Mészáros, chapter 2.) Various human efforts to stem the flow of lava, once in motion, have usually met with little success.

It is here suggested that a nuclear bomb of the order of 1–10 kT penetrating 100 m or so into an active volcano could initiate an explosive eruption of lava or gases and perhaps instigate a violent injection of dust into the atmosphere. By way of example, one might note that the USA contains, among numerous others, at least eight major active volcanoes: Mount St Helens (southern Washington state), Mount Baker (north-western Washington state), Mount Rainier (west-central Washington state), Mount Hood (north-western Oregon), Lassen Peak (north-eastern California), Mount Augustine (coastal southern Alaska), Mount Katmai (southern Alaska) and Mauna Loa (including Kilauea) (south-central Hawaii Island, Hawaii). A quiescent volcano would be especially vulnerable to triggering during some period preceding an eruption. It appears that whether or not an eruption is imminent can now be recognized (i.e., monitored) by remote seismic instruments (Qamar et al., 1983; Weaver et al., 1983) and thus the brief period when it would be especially 'ripe' for hostile manipulation.

Breaching of water containments

Flooding has been employed in warfare on many occasions, sometimes with catastrophic loss of life, agricultural damage and environmental disruption (Westing, 1977, pages 54–55; see also Westing, chapter 1, section IV).

Especially likely targets would be key dams and similar river-control systems which provide hydroelectric power and irrigation systems on a large scale. For example, the Colorado River system in western USA consists of seven major dams for river control, electrical generation and water supply to an arid region for domestic and agricultural purposes (Sibley, 1977). This system supplies water and power to almost 10 per cent of the land area of the USA and supports a regional population of some 17 million. A feasible, and perhaps the most dramatic, opportunity for lithospheric modification in the USA would be the destruction of the Glen Canyon dam in northern Arizona, the master dam or linchpin in the system.

The Mississippi River, the principal river of the USA, has been silting up its course (and thereby raising the elevation of its bed) as a consequence of natural geomorphic processes. The present course of the river has been assiduously maintained for many decades by constant and elaborate construction and repair of levees and dikes. The river had been accustomed to changing the course of its lower reaches one or more times every few thousand years, a now overdue event. Hostile disruption of the precarious equilibrium being maintained by the river's artificial containment system about 150 km north of its mouth—a readily feasible action—would instantly change the course of the river (into the Atchafalaya River valley) with catastrophic consequences. Such a lithospheric modification would bring about extensive flooding in Louisiana, would end the role of New Orleans as a major city, would disturb oil and gas production along the Louisiana (Gulf of Mexico) coast and would adversely affect agriculture and industry over a great area.

Melting of polar ice

It has been suggested authoritatively that especially the so-called West Antarctic ice sheet is inherently unstable and could be caused to disintegrate by mechanisms unrelated to climatic change (Hughes, 1975; Thomas, 1976; Weertman, 1976). The Byrd glacier is potentially unstable and, were the Ross ice shelf removed, this glacier would flow out to sea rather rapidly (Hughes and Fastook, 1981). Such an occurrence would result in a world-wide rise in sea level of about 5 m (Mercer, 1978). A rise in sea level of this magnititude would not only wreak havoc to the coastlines and adjacent land areas throughout the world, but would probably also bring about major regional changes in temperature and rainfall. Among the few beneficiaries of such a drastic environmental modification might be a number of equatorial African countries.

It is conceivable that a single 1 MT nuclear bomb dropped on the Byrd glacier near its entrance to the Ross ice shelf might be able to accomplish such a modification. Causing Mount Erebus, an active volcano on an island in the Ross Sea, to erupt explosively (see below) might also place in jeopardy the regional ice sheet.

Disruption of permafrost soils

Some 800 million hectares of the arctic regions of the world—especially in northern North America, Europe and Asia—and thus about 5 per cent of the global land surface, support a tundra vegetation that grows in so-called permafrost soil, the year-round freezing depth of which exceeds its depth of summer thaw (Westing, 1980, pages 114–117). The horizon that thaws, referred to as the active layer, averages somewhat less than 2 m in depth (range, approximately 0–4 m).

The tundra vegetation is exceedingly slow to renew itself, once disturbed. In Alaska, for example, there remain major scars in the plant cover that have changed little in the three decades since the vegetation was scraped away during oil exploration and development. Such disturbance disrupts the stability of the permafrost, leading to profound changes in the local habitat. Moreover, by altering the reflectivity of the surface there is an influence on the regional heat balance and thus on the regional pattern of air circulation and climate.

A nuclear bomb set off as a low air burst would destroy the tundra vegetation—and thus disrupt the environment—over a huge area for an indefinite period of time.

III. Conclusion

A number of geospheric instabilities have been summarized here which might conceivably lend themselves to manipulations with hostile intent. It is difficult to rank all of these divers possibilities in terms of the likelihood of their being usable. This is the case for a number of reasons, among them: (a) the magnitude of instability is often difficult to ascertain; (b) the ease with which it can be triggered is often difficult to assess; and (c) there may be seasonal variabilities in the instability or unpredictable long-term changes in it.

Manipulations of the lithosphere that would be relatively easy to achieve include the release of contained water (by rupturing dams, dikes and levees with either conventional or nuclear weapons), the transitory liquefaction of thixotropic soils (by instigating subsurface tremors with nuclear weapons) and the activation of volcanoes which are on the verge of eruption (by rupturing their interiors with nuclear weapons). Manipulations that would be difficult to achieve include the melting of polar ice sheets and the triggering of earthquakes, the latter whether on land or on the seabed. Clearly the most likely form of environmental warfare to be waged that involves manipulations of the geosphere would be the destruction of major inland river systems or coastal dikes.

Finally, it is important to point out that the adverse consequences of environmental modification involving the geosphere can be substantial, long-lasting and—most importantly—unpredictable. Even the civil modifications carried out in unhurried times of peace and with good intent often turn out to be catastrophic blunders. The Vaiont dam disaster has already been alluded to, and numerous others could be enumerated (see, e.g., Griggs and Gilchrist, 1983). If we are so readily capable of underestimating natural hazards in the course of peaceful development, we will be virtually certain to miscalculate the magnitude and longevity of the consequences of environmental modification as an act of war.

References

Bolt, B. A. 1976. *Nuclear Explosions and Earthquakes: The Parted Veil.* San Francisco: W. H. Freeman, 309 pp.

Boucher, G., Ryall, A. and Jones, A. E. 1969. Earthquakes associated with underground nuclear explosions. *Journal of Geophysical Research*, Washington, 74: 3808-3820.

Clark, W. H. 1961. Chemical and thermonuclear explosives. *Bulletin of the Atomic Scientists*, Chicago, 17: 356-360.

Emiliani, C., Harrison, C. G. A. and Swanson, M. 1969. Underground nuclear explosions and the control of earthquakes. *Science*, Washington, 165: 1255-1265.

Fedotov, S. A. and Markhinin, Y. K. (eds). 1983. *Great Tolbachik Fissure Eruption: Geological and Geophysical Data 1975-1976.* New York: Cambridge University Press, 341 pp.

Griggs, G. B. and Gilchrist, J. A. 1983. *Geologic Hazards, Resources, and Environmental Planning.* 2nd ed. Belmont, Cal.: Wadsworth, 502 pp.

Hughes, T. 1975. West Antarctic ice sheet: instability, disintegration, and initiation of ice ages. *Reviews of Geophysics and Space Physics*, Washington, 13: 502-526.

Hughes, T. and Fastook, J. L. 1981. Byrd glacier: 1978-1979 field results. *Antarctic Journal of the United States*, Washington, 16(5): 86-89.

Keefer, D. K. 1984. Rock avalanches caused by earthquakes: source characteristics. *Science*, Washington, 223: 1288-1290.

Kerr, R. A. 1983. Harbingers of the Coalinga earthquake. *Science*, Washington, 222: 918.

Kerr, R. A. 1984. Stalking the next Parkfield earthquake. *Science*, Washington, 223: 36-38.

Lange, G. J. de. 1983. Geochemical evidence of a massive slide in the southern Norwegian sea. *Nature*, London, 305: 420-422.

MacDonald, G. J. F. 1968. How to wreck the environment. In: Calder, N. (ed.). *Unless Peace Comes: A Scientific Forecast of New Weapons.* London: Allen Lane, 217 pp.: pp. 165-183.

Mercer, J. H. 1978. West Antarctic ice sheet and CO_2 greenhouse effect: a threat of disaster. *Nature*, London, 271: 321-325.

Noltimier, H. C. 1974. Geophysics of the north Atlantic basin. In: Nairn, A. E. M. and Stehli, F. G. (eds). *Ocean Basins and Margins. II. The North Atlantic.* New York: Plenum, 598 pp.: pp. 539-588 + 2 figs.

Oakeshott, G. B. 1976. *Volcanoes & Earthquakes: Geologic Violence.* New York: McGraw-Hill, 143 pp.

Prior, D. B., Coleman, J. M. and Doyle, E. H. 1984. Antiquity of the continental slope along the middle-Atlantic margin of the United States. *Science*, Washington, 223: 926-928.

Qamar, A., St. Lawrence, W., Moore, J. N. and Kendrick, G. 1983. Seismic signals preceeding the explosive eruption of Mount St. Helens, Washington, on 18 May 1980. *Bulletin of the Seismological Society of America*, Berkeley, Cal., 74(A): 1797-1813.

Sibley, G. 1977. Desert empire. *Harper's*, New York, 255(1529): 49-68.

Thomas, R. H. 1976. Thickening of the Ross ice shelf and equilibrium state of the west Antarctic ice sheet. *Nature*, London, 259: 180-183.

Weaver, C. S., Zollweg, J. E. and Malone, S. D. 1983. Deep earthquakes beneath Mount St. Helens: evidence for magmatic gas transport? *Science*, Washington, 221: 1391-1394.

Weertman, J. 1976. Glaciology's grand unsolved problem. *Nature*, London, 260: 284-286.

Westing, A. H. 1977. Geophysical and environmental weapons. In: SIPRI (eds). *Weapons of Mass Destruction and The Environment.* London: Taylor & Francis, 95 pp.: chap. 3 (pp. 49-63).

Westing, A. H. 1980. In: SIPRI (eds). *Warfare in a Fragile World: Military Impact on the Human Environment.* London: Taylor & Francis, 249 pp.

4. Environmental disruption by military means and international law

Richard A. Falk
Princeton University

1. Introduction

The recent attention devoted to the long-term effects of nuclear war, the cumulative impact of which has become popularly described as the 'nuclear winter', has for the first time dramatized to the public the distinct menace of environmental disruption resulting from military activities (A. Ehrlich, 1984; P. Ehrlich, 1984; P. Ehrlich *et al.*, 1983; Sagan, 1983–84; Turco *et al.*, 1983). Thomas (1983–84, pages 993–994) speculates about the overall circumstance of survival in a post-attack setting: "In such an event, the question of the survival of human beings becomes almost a trivial one. To be sure, some might get through, even live on, but under conditions infinitely more hostile to humans than those that existed one or two million years ago when our species first made its appearance." Given the magnitude and possibly irreversible character of the disruption resulting from any extensive use of nuclear weapons, it becomes absurd to view and dismiss such environmental disruption as incidental.

Despite acknowledgement of this menace, to turn to international law for relief provides only the most scant basis for hope at present. As has been observed in relation to the Environmental Modification (Enmod) Convention of 1977 (for the text of the Convention, see appendix 2, section III), seemingly only those techniques of environmental modification beyond the scope of 'rational' war making have been forbidden (Goldblat, 1982, page 53). What is militarily attractive remains permissible, or at least not explicitly prohibited, whereas that which is of no evident relevance to war making is diligently proscribed. Incredibly, not even the chain of deliberate military activities associated with inducing a 'nuclear winter' is outlawed by the Enmod Convention because, presumably, the direct intention of nuclear attack would be the destruction of enemy capabilities, not the induced chain of environmental 'side-effects' which cumulatively produce the period of adverse weather conditions.

In a sense, the entire law of war exists uneasily within this problematic setting.

Representatives of states are unwilling to agree upon explicit prohibitions that encroach upon their freedom of action in wartime. As a result, especially those governments that have relied upon tactics of environmental disruption in the past are reluctant to acknowledge the dubious character of their earlier policies and to constrain their choice of military options in the future. At the same time, the force of public opinion creates pressure to do something that acknowledges growing concerns about the character and consequence of war. Hence, there is a steady stream of agreements and conferences bearing on the development of law governing the various aspects of armed conflict. The point here is not to deny the validity of such undertakings, but to take note of their inability to overcome an absence of political will by governments to oppose war making, even at the self-destructive upper limits of nuclear war making.

Often the official justification for this resistance to law making has to do with the insufficiency of verification and enforcement techniques. In effect, since the 'other' side cannot be trusted it is necessary to possess offsetting capabilities. This kind of reasoning underlies the rationale for the policy of nuclear deterrence, as well as for the accompanying nuclear arms race.

Closely linked to this argument is the contention that the relative humaneness of tactical choices cannot be helpfully laid down in advance. The claim, for instance, that the use of atomic bombs in 1945 against Japanese cities 'saved lives' and ended World War II more rapidly is a prominent example of such reasoning, although its specific factual premises have been increasingly challenged by recent scholarship. More pertinently, perhaps, military planners in the USA are resistant to prohibitions on 'useful' military options that involve deliberate environmental destruction of the sorts resorted to in the Second Indochina War (Westing, 1976). This concept of legitimate military necessity is a particularly powerful obstacle to law making where, as here, there exists no logic of reciprocity to make adoption of restraints seem worthwhile to powerful, high-technology states. In counter-insurgency warfare, the natural environment provides cover and protection to the insurgent side, but it impedes the efforts of the counter-insurgent side to 'cleanse' the countryside.

The general record of compliance with international law in major wars has not been encouraging. The dictates of military necessity, as assessed by opposed leaderships, have taken consistent precedence over the laws of war in almost every critical aspect of belligerent policy. Thus, in World War II unrestricted air and submarine warfare overcame earlier explicit rules on neutral rights and duties embodied in the 1907 Hague Conventions V and XIII (Roberts and Guelff, 1982, pages 61 and 109), as well as even more fundamental prohibitions upon waging war directly against civilian targets. Indeed, the concept of 'total war', evolving through the two world wars, supported without serious qualms the deliberate destruction of entire cities from the air and raised questions about whether it was at all possible to regulate the conduct of war in meaningful respects. Tendencies towards unconditional warfare with increasingly destructive and indiscriminate weaponry and doctrine were growing on all sides. These negative observations should be qualified in certain ways. To some extent, the relevance of the rules of law to warfare were rehabilitated and reaffirmed by the Nuremberg judgements of the United Nations War Crimes Commission (UNWCC, 1948) and by subsequent negotiations designed to modernize and extend the law of armed conflict. Additionally, some of the latest innovations in weapon technology, both at nuclear and conventional levels, emphasize accuracy, facilitating discrimination among targets; partly in response to earlier criticism, these innovations are accompanied by new military doctrines calling for such discrimination. These developments are troublesome in other respects, seemingly lending some level of legitimacy (moral, legal, cultural) to reliance by the state upon a nuclear option (Brooklyn, 1983; Builder and Graubard, 1982; Falk, 1983; Weston, 1983).

The standard obstacles to effective law making noted above are made even more impassable by some special features of the current international setting. Overall, this is not a favourable time to initiate additional law-making initiatives. There is a keen scepticism about adherence to existing explicit prohibitions, for instance, with respect to chemical weaponry. There have been significant recent accusations directed at both the USSR and Viet Nam, and at Iraq (in the current Iraq–Iran War), of illegal use of chemical weapons of various kinds, a context within which the legal prohibition is regarded as firm. Beyond this, a series of combat circumstances disclose an absence of respect for well-established rules contained in the law of war (MacBride *et al.*, 1983). More general still is the overall hostility to a law-oriented approach to foreign policy associated with the current US presidency. It must be acknowledged, however, that this shift in attitude by the USA from principal champion of the development of international law to prominent opponent influences the whole international atmosphere with respect to such undertakings. The belated and precipitous withdrawal by the USA in 1982 from the Law of the Sea Treaty negotiations and its extraordinary suspension in April 1984 of accountability for two years to the International Court of Justice (delivered on the virtual eve of Nicaragua's submission of a legal complaint) struck momentous, although perhaps temporary, symbolic and substantive blows to the rule of law in world affairs.

In these contexts of law making that involve high-technology warfare in the Third World or the regulation of weapons of mass destruction at the technological frontier, it is difficult to achieve meaningful agreements in the traditional sense of inter-governmental participation without the support of the USA. It may still be worthwhile to press forward with law making, but then the goal needs to be associated with the strengthening of public opinion more than with the promoting of rules and procedures that are likely to serve as effective regulators of state practice.

Also relevant is the realization that creating rules and procedures does not by itself ensure their serious utilization. After years of effort, an agreed definition of aggression under the United Nations Charter was finally achieved in 1974 (UNGA, 1974b), but its impact on subsequent state practice has been virtually nil. Finding ways of making existing legal arrangements more effective and creating new legal arrangements are part of the challenge. In the environmental context, however, it is true that the norms directly available, with the partial exception of the Enmod Convention, are very general; more detailed prescriptions would be useful, as would the process of their negotiation.

Indirect norms, by way of general international law of war, provide an existing framework that, if energetically interpreted and implemented, would protect the environment against military activities. These general, indirect rules and procedures, although suggestive of the direction of further development, derive from general principles that are not treated by governments as inhibiting or guiding their specific actions very significantly. At the same time, their existence does provide some criteria by which to appraise the legality of controversial policies harmful to the environment. Such a general framework is no substitute for invigorating the treaty process for environmental subject matter. Part of the challenge of making international law effective is to make governments and political leaders feel as if they have given their consent in a formal and active process of negotiation and accession (signature and ratification).

II. Emergent international law

International law did not regard environmental protection as a distinct goal of the law of war until the upsurge of specific environmental concerns in the 1970s. Military activities were not perceived as posing any special threat to environmental quality, although, in fact, various tactics of scorched earth and crop destruction throughout the history of warfare did serious local environmental harm, and there were occasional expressions of concern all along about injuries done to animals or prized environmental surroundings.

To be sure, safeguarding belligerent property interests unwittingly included an element of environmental protection. Thus the 1907 Hague Convention IV Respecting the Laws and Customs of War on Land states in article 55 that (Roberts and Guelff, 1982, page 57):

The occupying State shall be regarded only as administrator and usufructary of public buildings, real estate, forests, and agricultural estates belonging to the hostile State, and situated in the occupied country. It must safeguard the capital of these properties, and administer them in accordance with the rules of usufruct.

This principle is carried forward in somewhat more straightforward property terms in the 1949 Geneva Convention IV Relative to the Protection of Civilian Persons in Time of War, stating in article 53 that (Roberts and Guelff, 1982, page 290):

Any destruction by the Occupying Power of real or personal property belonging individually or collectively to private persons, or to the State, or to other public authorities, or to social or cooperative organizations, is prohibited, except where such destruction is rendered absolutely necessary by military operations.

It is difficult to assess whether such guidelines were operative in constraining belligerent occupation, but, as stressed, the protection of the environment as such was incidental to the purpose of such legal rules. The neglect of the environment as a distinct concern was consistent with the overall view of Western civilization that nature existed solely for the glory of humankind. International law, in its formative period, reflected this anti-nature bias of our civilization.

Flagrant disregard of these restraints was the basis for charges of war crimes against 10 German civilian administrators of Polish forests during a period of belligerent occupation (1939–44) in the course of World War II. Nine of these Germans were accused of war crimes by the United Nations War Crimes Commission at Nuremberg (its case no. 7150) because of their implementation of a Nazi policy "of ruthless exploitation of Polish forestry", which was treated as "pillaging", and involved "the wholesale cutting of Polish timber to an extent far in excess of what was necessary to preserve the timber resources of the country" (UNWCC, 1948, page 496). In this passage there is recognized a legal right pertaining to sustaining the resource base, at least in the context of occupation. Note that article 53 of the 1949 Geneva Convention IV (quoted above) permits a belligerent to destroy property to the extent "rendered absolutely necessary by military operations". Once such a criterion is introduced it confines the legal prohibition to wanton or superfluous destruction. Such judgements of necessity are difficult to second-guess; hence, the regulatory effects are likely to be modest. Only in retrospect, and then by victors in relation to the deeds of losers in a war, would wanton destruction of natural surroundings or resources seem to create a basis for legal accountability. By then, the damage would have been done. In the next war, the nature of the modern state reaffirms its claims of unconditional national security interests, leading to the primacy of military necessity and the disregard of environmentally disruptive effects. More substantial restraint might result, however, if the necessity exception were to be more self-consciously restricted to *lawful* military operations by leaders and planners.

There was remarkably little concern about environmental destruction *per se* until the Second Indochina War. Efforts to place the issue of military activities on the agenda of the United Nations Conference on the Human Environment, held in Stockholm in 1972, were not successful, largely because of US objections arising from its sensitivity to criticism directed at its then current practices of environmental destruction during the Second Indochina War. An informal counter-conference was held in Stockholm at the same time as the official conference in order to highlight the importance of this *political* oversight, and to consider the environmental harm associated with counter-insurgency war and its legal status (Falk, 1973). The prime minister of Sweden did usefully call public attention to the problem of environmental destruction in Indochina, and also within the context of testing and uses of nuclear weaponry.

Nevertheless, the Conference Declaration in its 'Proclamation' section avoided associating serious environmental dangers explicitly with military activities. However, in its 'Principles' section there is a direct acknowledgement of environmental threats posed by nuclear and other weapons of mass destruction. Principle 26 of the Declaration reads (UNGA, 1973b, page 5):

Man and his environment must be spared the effects of nuclear weapons and all other means of mass destruction. States must strive to reach prompt agreement, in the relevant international organs, on the elimination and complete destruction of such weapons.

Principle 21 of the Declaration seeks to reconcile sovereign rights with environmental protection (UNGA, 1973b, page 5):

States have, in accordance with the Charter of the United Nations and the principles of international law, the sovereign right to exploit their own resources pursuant to their own environmental policies, and the responsibility to ensure that activities within their jurisdiction or control do not cause damage to the environment of other States or of areas beyond the limits of national jurisdiction.

Such a principle may embody customary international law and therefore express an obligation that does, in theory, apply to military activities with transnational effects, especially those whose harmful environmental effects are not confined to belligerent countries. Subsequent United Nations General Assembly resolutions recognized the need for more explicitness. A resolution on the 'Effects of atomic radiation' deplored the polluting effects being caused by the continued atmospheric testing of nuclear weapons (UNGA, 1973a). Another, on the 'Prohibition of action to influence the environment...', considered "it necessary to adopt, through the conclusion of an appropriate international convention, effective measures to prohibit action to influence the environment and climate for military and other hostile purposes, which are incompatible with the maintenance of international security, human well-being and health" (UNGA, 1974a).

These background sentiments more forcefully animate the 1982 World Charter for Nature adopted by the United Nations General Assembly by a vote of 118 in favour and 1 against (with 18 abstentions) (UNGA, 1982). In its first operative section, devoted to 'General principles', paragraph 5 is pertinent: "Nature shall be secured against degradation caused by warfare or other hostile activities". In a separate section of 'Functions', paragraph 11 seems relevant:

Activities which might have an impact on nature shall be controlled, and the best available technologies that minimize significant risks to nature or other adverse effects shall be used; in particular:
 (a) Activities which are likely to cause irreversible damage to nature shall be avoided;
 (b) Activities which are likely to pose a significant risk to nature shall be preceded by an exhaustive examination; their proponents shall demonstrate that expected benefits outweigh potential damage to nature, and where potential adverse effects are not fully understood, the activities should not proceed.

These formulations, given assent by representatives of governments after careful drafting, discussion and reflection, are certainly indicative of an emerging consensus that would seem to forbid reliance on all forms of direct and indirect assaults on the environment in the course of a war effort. Yet there is no political capacity to make such implications explicit. It is also noteworthy that the one negative vote cast against the World Charter for Nature was by the USA, the state that has relied on large-scale, systematic environmental warfare in a recent conflict. Several states, indeed all of the nuclear powers, insist on retaining options relating to testing, threats and uses of nuclear weaponry, although several, including China and the USSR, have formally renounced first-use options. Hence, the direction of international normative thought is clear, but it lacks authoritativeness in that the most evident policy implications are avoided; and the perhaps most significant state relative to normative developments refuses to endorse even these abstract formulations of the principles at stake.

The 1977 Protocol I Additional to the 1949 Geneva Conventions is also relevant to these assessments (for the text of the Protocol, see appendix 3). This Protocol carried forward the earlier general directives on environmental protection against military activities. It elaborates on some of the general thinking embodied in the 1899 and 1907 Hague Conventions and in article 35 sets forth the following standards of law (Roberts and Guelff, 1982, page 409):

1. In any armed conflict, the right of the Parties to the conflict to choose methods or means of warfare is not unlimited.

2. It is prohibited to employ weapons, projectiles and material and methods of warfare of a nature to cause superfluous injury or unnecessary suffering.

3. It is prohibited to employ methods or means of warfare which are intended, or may be expected, to cause widespread, long-term and severe damage to the natural environment.

On the face of it, article 35.3 would seem to prohibit weapons of mass destruction, yet this is far from assured. The legal reach of the formulations is restricted, or at least ambiguous, because the US delegate to the negotiations had insisted that this Protocol not be understood as intending to have any bearing on the legal status of nuclear weapons. In question here is whether the formulation in article 35.3 is merely expressive of international customary law, and thus cannot be restricted in its scope by the unilateral declaration of any government. Article 36, dealing with new weapons, is also relevant inasmuch as it implies that a new weapon may be illegal even if not subject to an explicit prohibition either by 'this Protocol or by any other rule of international law''. At the same time experts on international law mainly agree that the legality of new weapons and tactics cannot be presumed, but depends on establishing compatibility with pre-existing general principles of the law of war (Carnegie Endowment, 1971, page 29).

The 1977 Geneva Protocol I expresses a rule in its article 55 that seems to incorporate the minimum current consensus of international law on military activities in relation to the natural environment (Roberts and Guelff, 1982, page 418):

1. Care shall be taken in warfare to protect the natural environment against widespread, long-term and severe damage. This protection includes a prohibition of the use of methods or means of warfare which are intended or may be expected to cause such damage to the natural environment and thereby prejudice the health or survival of the population.

2. Attacks against the natural environment by way of reprisal are prohibited.

Note here that this formulation does not clearly prohibit the type of tactics relied upon by the USA in the Second Indochina War, which could arguably fall below the damage threshold of "widespread, long-term and severe". However, it might well be that an impartial tribunal, if convened to assess environmental harm in Indochina, would find US practices incompatible with the standards of article 55. In the so-called Understanding relating to article I of the 1977 Enmod Convention the terms 'widespread', 'long-lasting' and 'severe' were interpreted as follows by the Conference of the Committee on Disarmament (CCD) (see appendix 2, section III):

(a) "widespread": encompassing an area on the scale of several hundred square kilometres;

(b) "long-lasting": lasting for a period of months, or approximately a season;

(c) "severe": involving serious or significant disruption or harm to human life, natural and economic resources or other assets.

The CCD stressed that this interpretation was 'intended exclusively for this Convention and is not intended to prejudice the interpretation of the same or similar terms if used in connexion with any other international agreement'.

One must note that these three criteria, as used in the 1977 Geneva Protocol I, are not subject to any exemption by way of military necessity, nor is the prohibition directed, as in the Enmod Convention, only at tactics that have as their object environmental destruction. At the same time, the word "and" rather than "or", as in the Enmod Convention, suggests that all three features of environmental harm must be present for the prohibition to be applicable. It would appear, by virtue of the textual language, that most contemplated uses of weaponry of mass destruction fall within the ban.

The general prohibition of article 55 of the 1977 Geneva Protocol I is made more specific in article 56 where "dams, dykes and nuclear electrical generating stations" are legally protected from attack "even where these objects are military objectives". In fact, article 56.1 even forbids attack upon "military objectives located at or in the vicinity of these works or installations . . . if such attack may cause the release of dangerous forces". Unfortunately this "special protection against attack" is partially withdrawn in article 56.2 where these installations, including dams, dikes and nuclear electrical generating stations, can be attacked if they are being used "in regular, significant and direct support of military operations and if such attack is the only feasible way to terminate such support". Whether this "special protection" will mean much, if anything, in the setting of war remains to be seen, but the recognition of these new environmental dimensions of the law of war is at least a formal acknowledgement of concern that can be acted upon by public pressures.

Whether such legal standards were applicable prior to 1977 depends on whether they are regarded as incorporating earlier treaty and customary rules of war, or as establishing something new. Note also that the 1981 Convention on Prohibitions or Restrictions on the Use of Certain Conventional Weapons confidently invokes in its preamble these recent legal developments of isolating environmental protection as a distinct concern of the international law of war (Roberts and Guelff, 1982, page 469): "*Also recalling* that it is prohibited to employ methods or means of warfare which are intended, or may be expected, to cause widespread, long-term and severe damage to the natural environment."

As has been emphasized, the attitude of the USA towards these issues is both crucial and troublesome. The Enmod Convention (for a detailed discussion of which see Goldblat, chapter 5) is constructed around this threshold notion of "widespread, long-lasting, or severe". It is worth noting the statement of the US Secretary of State at the time the USA signed this Convention. On that occasion, this formal statement indicated that "The United States will be prepared to re-examine this limitation on the scope of the convention at the review conference or possibly before" (Vance, 1977, page 634). Even if such a threshold were to be removed it would restrict the applicability to environmental warfare *per se*. It would still not reach the problems associated with long-term environmental effects of nuclear and other weapons of mass destruction.

A final set of observations is needed in order to clarify the extent to which treaty law is not exhaustive of the content of the international law of war. There is no doubt that the codification conferences at the Hague in 1899 and 1907, as well as such subsequent efforts in Geneva in 1949 and 1977, arose in relation to a pre-existing set of rules of customary international law (patterns of practice performed with a sense of obligation), as well as with notions of natural law (norms of behaviour binding on all levels of social organization without any particular manifestation of a consent to be bound). More recently, in addition, there has come to exist the idea of a community competence to legislate binding norms by consensus (or overwhelming vote). The grave limitation of these sources of law is that they are not operationally binding, it seems, on political leaders, military planners or others who act on behalf of the state. At the same time, these legal directives should not be neglected. They point to the directions which public efforts to influence international behaviour should take. Also, by providing a kind of legal underpinning, they accord public demands for restraint with an aura of legitimacy, justifying, it would seem, certain forms of opposition, or even resistance, by individuals, groups and international institutions, to official policies and practices of state.

A most important concept embedded in 'unwritten' international law was set forth in the so-called de Martens clause found in the preamble to the 1899 Hague Convention II, and essentially repeated in the preamble to the 1907 Hague Convention IV, the latter version presented here (Roberts and Guelff, 1982, page 45):

Until a more complete code of the laws of war has been issued, the high contracting Parties deem it expedient to declare that, in cases not included in the Regulations adopted by them, the inhabitants and the belligerents remain under the protection and the rule of the principles of the law of nations, as they result from the usages established among civilized peoples, from the laws of humanity, and the dictates of the public conscience.

Again, this orientation towards applicability beyond the orbit of consent is carried forward in a provision contained in each of the four 1949 Geneva Conventions on the humanitarian side of the law of war, as well as in the two 1977 Protocols additional to the 1949 Geneva Conventions and in the 1981 Convention on Conventional Weapons (for the texts of these Conventions, see Roberts and Guelff, 1982). It would seem plausible to argue that a fair reading of this language is irreconcilable with any legal role for weaponry of mass destruction. Note particularly that such a concern is wider than nuclear weaponry and extends to biological, chemical and radiological weapons as well as to some emerging categories of conventional weapons.

Also relevant here is the general international-law prohibition on intervention in the internal affairs of sovereign states, a norm that is almost logically mandated by the existence of a world of states each of which claims territorial sovereignty. There are a variety of indications, enjoying varying degrees of confirmation, that covert operations directed at foreign societies that include hostile activities have been directed at cash crops and the like. Extensive hearings on the US Central Intelligence Agency (CIA) in the US Senate a few years ago investigated, among many other intelligence abuses, "the illegal possession of deadly biological poisons which were retained within the CIA for 5 years after their destruction was ordered by the President, and for 5 years after the United States had entered into a solemn international commitment not to maintain stocks of these poisons except for very limited research purposes" (Church, 1975, page 2). It seems evident that covert operations harmful to the natural environment of a foreign country are prohibited by the non-intervention norm, for instance as set forth in detailed form by the United Nations General Assembly (UNGA, 1965), but the effective implementation of this norm requires intensifying the overall cultural inhibition that acts upon doing deliberate harm to the natural environment. International law, standing by itself, is not very helpful unless its content is reinforced by widely supported cultural norms.

Roberts and Guelff (1982, page 5) assert correctly that, "Perhaps the most fundamental customary principle is that the right of belligerents to adopt means of injuring the enemy is not unlimited". They point out that this notion was adopted by the 1874 Brussels Declaration and was formally codified in the 1899 Hague Convention II and the 1907 Hague Convention IV. This latter treaty provides an authoritative statement of the principle in its article 22 (Roberts and Guelff, 1982, page 52). The United Nations War Crimes Commission in the so-called Nuremberg judgement of 1946 held that the 1907 Hague Conventions as such were declaratory of the laws and customs of war, and hence binding on all states, whether or not they were parties who had given formal consent.

These notions are relevant and important for two reasons. First of all, such a framework establishes a legal context that makes calls for extensions of the law of war to the subject matter of environmental protection a matter of implementation, rather than of innovation. Second, 'public conscience' is authoritatively acknowledged as a source of law and policy guidance, making such instruments as the World Charter for Nature more legally operative than generally supposed. Third, the crystallization of 'public conscience' through the activities of informal groups and non-state initiatives is relevant to discerning the content of *existing* international law. In essence, the state cannot altogether defeat the formation of international law by withholding its consent.

III. Conclusion

As indicated, the case for legal development of environmental protection against military activities is overwhelming, yet the prospects are rather bleak. It can be confidently asserted that there exists "evidence of the general opinion that the protection of the environment belongs to the recognized principles of the laws of armed conflict" (Röling and Suković, 1976, page 40). In addition, there is the more specific, yet limited undertaking set forth in the Enmod Convention. Considering both the opportunities and inherent constraints likely to accompany the Enmod Convention review conference (September 1984), several directions of effort, in addition to the removal (or perhaps lowering) of threshold requirements by way of treaty amendment, seem constructive.

To argue to this effect, it should be stressed, is not to offer immediately relevant means to strengthen the international legal order. But recalling the law-creating role of "public conscience", wider efforts are appropriate, both to reflect the levels of concern that exist and to bring pressure to bear on the military policies of governments in the leading states. Four types of emphasis are suggested in summary form.

1. Prohibitions and limitations on the threat and use of nuclear weapons

There is a growing body of expert commentary and lawyers' concern with the status of nuclear weapons under international law (Falk, 1983; Weston, 1983). Also, there are a variety of public pressures to re-align strategic doctrine away from its current levels of dependence on nuclear weaponry, thereby making relevant legal undertakings of even a declaratory character—for instance, declarations of no-first-use of nuclear weapons. Other developments in monitoring technology (the so-called transparency revolution) and drastic or abolitionist variants of minimum deterrence, offer humanity some realistic grounds to hope for and to demand nuclear disarmament (Deudney, 1983; Schell, 1984). It is hardly necessary to emphasize that no single step will be more supportive of environmental quality than reductions in the risk that nuclear weapons will be used, especially on a large scale (i.e., in excess of say, 100 MT). Other weapons of mass destruction and a variety of emerging weapon technologies also pose serious threats of environmental disruption.

2. International environmental impact statements on military activities and capabilities

There is a definite need to facilitate public awareness in the context of environmental harm arising from military activities and capabilities. A useful contribution, building possibly on existing customary legal norms, would be an annual review of the environmental impact of military activities and capabilities. Such an effort could probably be undertaken most usefully at this stage by a non-governmental scientific organization of widely recognized high standing (see also Krass, chapter 6).

3. Formulation and advocacy of a convention on ecocide

A proposal for a convention on ecocide derives its inspiration from the successful adoption of the 1948 Convention on the Prevention and Punishment of the Crime of Genocide (Roberts and Guelff, 1982, pages 157–168). The Genocide Convention became incorporated explicitly into international law, in the aftermath of the Nazi holocaust—largely, it might be noted, through the devoted efforts of a single individual, Raphael Lemkin (Kuper, 1981, pages 22–23). Alas, acts of genocide continue. However, the criminal character of genocide has been confirmed, a reality that lends a measure of support to all international efforts on behalf of the victims of genocide.

To formulate and promote a parallel convention with reference to deliberate, systematic environmental destruction would itself be educative (Falk, 1973). To the extent that governments could be induced to adhere to such a convention, it might draw into question within military bureaucracies practices and capabilities having an objective of environmental destruction. At the very least, designating ecocide as a crime of state would contribute to the hardening of cultural norms on safeguarding the environment and would thereby give content to the law-generative notion of 'public conscience'. A possible text of a Convention on the Crime of Ecocide is provided in order to convey a clearer sense of content (annex 4.1).

4. Formation of cultural norms in opposition to military activities that cause direct or indirect environmental harm

The analogy to the movement against nuclear weaponry is relevant in considering the normative underpinnings related to environmental disruption. Religious bodies, in particular, have both reflected and contributed cultural norms in opposition to the military policies and practices of nuclear weapon states (Blackaby *et al.*, 1984, pages 3–6; Heyer, 1982). The pastoral letter of US Catholic bishops on nuclear weapons issued in 1983 exerted an enormous impact on public opinion, undermining societal support for the logic of deterrence and the nuclear arms race (Bernardin *et al.*, 1983). The emergent cultural consensus against nuclear weapons also stimulates interpretative efforts and the level of concern about legal status.

It would seem appropriate to stimulate a comparable societal movement with respect to environmental issues. The 1972 Declaration of the United Nations Conference on the Human Environment and the 1982 World Charter for Nature move in this direction within international forums. More specificity of analysis and prescription could facilitate serious questioning of governmental policies. In this respect, a pastoral letter or encyclical on the sacred character of the human environment could powerfully reinforce secular efforts as well as make an independent contribution. The civilizational stance on nature, as has often been pointed out, is profoundly problematical, even in biblical contexts. The case for authoritative clarification of cultural norms can only improve the atmosphere within which other more formal and technical efforts are made. Governments are staffed by human beings sensitive to shifts in normative settings and cultural attitudes. The time is ripe to sharpen the tensions between cultural norms protective of the environment and military activities threatening to it.

Annex 4.1. A proposed Convention on the Crime of Ecocide

The following draft of a proposed Convention on the Crime of Ecocide is the revision of an earlier draft by the author (Falk, 1973, pages 14–16):

The Contracting Parties,
   Recalling and reaffirming an emerging disposition by the governments of the world to protect the natural environment against deliberate destruction by human actions, are determined to take a further step to realize the goals of the Declaration of the 1972 Conference on the Human Environment, of the United Nations General Assembly Resolution No. 3154(XXVIII) of 14 December 1973 and of the 1982 World Charter for Nature;
   Acting on the belief that ecocide is a crime under international law, contrary to the spirit and aims of the United Nations, and condemned by peoples and governments of good will throughout the world;
   Recognizing that we are living in a period of increasing danger of ecological collapse;
   Acknowledging that humans have consciously and unconsciously inflicted irreparable damage on the environment in times of both war and peace;
   Being convinced that the pursuit of ecological quality requires international guidelines to establish the content of international responsibility and procedures for co-operation and enforcement;
   Being concerned that recent advances in technological capacity and scientific knowledge virtually assure an expanding ability to modify the environment in serious respects and that it is timely to act now in order to repudiate hostile activities against the environment; and, finally
   Being mindful of our responsibilities to present and future generations and also of the fact that the protection of the environment from hostile activities constitutes a critical current challenge;
   Hereby agree that:

Article I

   The Contracting Parties confirm that ecocide, whether committed in time of peace or in time of war, is a crime under international law which they undertake to prevent and to punish.

Article II

   In the present Convention, ecocide means any of the following acts committed with intent to disrupt or destroy, in whole or in part, a human ecosystem:

(a) The use of weapons of mass destruction, whether nuclear, bacteriological, chemical or other;

(b) The use of any explosive or weapon to provoke or intensify such natural disasters as volcanoes, earthquakes and floods;

(c) The use of chemical herbicides to defoliate and destroy natural forests for military purposes;

(d) The use of bombs and artillery in such quantity, density or size as to impair the quality of the soil or to enhance the prospect of diseases dangerous to human beings, animals or crops;

(e) The use of bulldozing or earth-moving equipment to destroy large tracts of forest or cropland for military purposes;

(f) The use of techniques designed to increase or decrease rainfall or otherwise modify weather and climate as a hostile act directed at a foreign state; and

(g) The forcible and permanent removal of human beings or animals from their habitual places of habitation on a large scale in order to expedite the pursuit of military or other objective.

Article III

The following acts shall be punishable:

(a) Ecocide;

(b) Conspiracy to commit ecocide;

(c) Direct and public incitement to ecocide;

(d) Attempt to commit ecocide; and

(e) Complicity in ecocide.

Article IV

Persons committing ecocide as defined in Article II or any of the acts described in Article III shall be punished, at least to the extent of being removed for a period of years from any position of leadership or public trust. Constitutionally responsible rulers, public officials, military commanders or private individuals may all be charged with and convicted of the crimes associated with ecocide as set forth in Article III.

Article V

The United Nations shall establish a Commission for the Investigation of Ecocide as soon as this Convention comes into force. The Commission shall be composed of 15 experts on international law and assisted by a staff conversant with ecology. The principal tasks of the Commission shall be to investigate allegations of ecocide whenever made by governments of States, by the principal officer of any international institution whether or not part of the United Nations system, by resolution of the United Nations General Assembly or United Nations Security Council or by petition signed by at least 1 000 private persons. The Commission shall have power of subpoena and to take depositions; all hearings of the Commission shall be open and transcripts of proceedings shall be a matter of public record. If after investigating the allegations, the Commission concludes by majority vote that none of the acts described in Article III has been committed, it shall issue a dismissal of the complaint accompanied by a short statement of reasons. If after investigating the allegations, the Commission concludes by majority vote that acts within the scope of Article III have been or are being committed, then it shall issue a cease and desist order, a statement recommending prosecution or sanction of specific individuals or groups, and a statement of reasons supporting its decision. It shall also recommend whether prosecution should proceed under national, regional, international or *ad hoc* auspices. Regardless of the decision, minority members of the Commission may attach dissenting or concurring opinions to the majority decision. In the event of a tie vote in the Commission, the Chairman shall cast a second vote. The Commission shall have rule-making capacity to regulate fully its operations to assure full realization of the objectives of this Convention but with due regard for the human rights embodied in the United Nations Declaration of Human Rights.

Article VI

The Contracting Parties undertake to enact, in accordance with their respective Constitutions, the necessary legislation to give effect to the provisions of the present Convention and, in particular, to provide effective penalties for persons guilty of ecocide or any of the other acts enumerated in Article III.

Article VII

Persons charged with ecocide or any other acts enumerated in Article III shall be tried by a competent tribunal of the State in the territory of which the act was committed, or by such international penal tribunal as may have jurisdiction with respect to those Contracting Parties which shall have accepted its jurisdiction.

Article VIII

Ecocide and the other acts enumerated in Article III shall not be considered as political crimes for the purpose of extradition.

The Contracting Parties pledge themselves in such cases to grant extradition in accordance with their laws and treaties in force.

Article IX

Any Contracting Party may call upon the competent organ of the United Nations to take such action under the Charter of the United Nations as it considers appropriate for the prevention and suppression of acts of ecocide or any of the other acts enumerated in Article III.

Article X

Disputes between the Contracting Parties relating to the interpretation, application or fulfilment of the present Convention, including those relating to the responsibility of a State for ecocide or any of the other acts enumerated in Article III, shall be submitted to the International Court of Justice at the request of any of the parties to the dispute.

Article XI

The present Convention, of which the Chinese, English, French, Russian and Spanish texts are equally authentic, shall bear the date of . . .

Article XII

The present Convention shall be open until . . . for signature on behalf of any Member of the United Nations and of any non-member State to which an invitation to sign has been addressed by the United Nations General Assembly.

The present Convention shall be ratified; and the instruments of ratification shall be deposited with the Secretary-General of the United Nations.

After the date of . . . the present Convention may be acceded to on behalf of any Member of the United Nations and of any non-member State which has received an invitiation as aforesaid.

Instruments of accession shall be deposited with the Secretary-General of the United Nations.

Article XIII

Any Contracting Party may at any time, by notification addressed to the Secretary-General of the United Nations, extend the application of the present Convention to all or any of the territories for the conduct of whose foreign relations that Contracting Party is responsible.

Article XIV

On the day when the first 20 instruments of ratification or accession have been deposited, the Secreary-General of the United Nations shall draw up a *procès verbal* and transmit a copy of it to each Member of the United Nations and to each of the non-member States contemplated in Article XII.

The present Convention shall come into force on the 90th day following the date of deposit of the 20th instrument of ratification or accession.

Any ratification of accession effected subsequent to the latter date shall become effective on the 90th day following the deposit of the instrument of ratification or accession.

Article XV

The present Convention shall remain in effect for a period of 10 years from the date of its coming into force.

It shall thereafter remain in force for successive periods of 5 years for such Contracting Parties as have not denounced it at least 6 months before the expiration of the current period.

Denunciation shall be effected by a written notification addressed to the Secretary-General of the United Nations.

Article XVI

If, as a result of denunciations, the number of Parties to the present Convention should become less than 16, the Convention shall cease to be in force as from the date on which the last of these denunciations shall become effective.

Article XVII

A request for the revision of the present Convention may be made at any time by any Contracting Party by means of a notification in writing addressed to the Secretary-General of the United Nations.

The United Nations General Assembly shall decide upon the steps, if any, to be taken in respect of such request.

Article XVIII

The Secretary-General of the United Nations shall notify all Members of the United Nations and the non-member States contemplated in Article XII of the following:

(*a*) Signatures, ratifications and accessions received in accordance with Article XII;

(*b*) Notifications received in accordance with Article XIII;

(*c*) The date on which the present Convention comes into force in accordance with Article XIV;

(*d*) Denunciations received in accordance with Article XV;

(*e*) The abrogation of the Convention in accordance with Article XVI; and

(*f*) Notifications received in accordance with Article XVII.

Article XIX

The original of the present Convention shall be deposited in the archives of the United Nations.

A certified copy of the Convention shall be transmitted to all Members of the United Nations and to the non-member States contemplated in Article XII.

Article XX

The present Convention shall be registered by the Secretary-General of the United Nations on the date of its coming into force.

References

Bernardin, J., Fulcher, G., Gumbleton, T., O'Connor, J. and Reilly, D. 1983. Challenge of peace: God's promise and our response [US bishops' pastoral letter on war and peace of 3 May 83]. *Origins*, Washington, **13**(1): 1–32.

Blackaby, F., Goldblat, J. and Lodgaard, S. 1984. No-first-use of nuclear weapons – an overview. In: Blackaby, F., Goldblat, J. and Lodgaard, S. (eds). *No-first-use*. London: Taylor & Francis, 151 pp.: pp. 3–26 [a SIPRI book].

Brooklyn. 1983. Nuclear weapons: a fundamental legal challenge. *Brooklyn Journal of International Law*, New York, **9**(2): 199–335.

Builder, C. H. and Graubard, M. H. 1982. *International Law of Armed Conflict: Implications for the Concept of Assured Destruction*. Santa Monica, Cal.: Rand Corporation Report No. R-2804-FF, 58 pp.

Carnegie Endowment (ed). 1971. *Law of Armed Conflicts*. New York: Carnegie Endowment for International Peace, 119 pp.

Church, F. (ed.). 1975. *Intelligence Activities: Senate Resolution 21. I. Unauthorized Storage of Toxic Agents* (Hearings, 16–18 Sep 75). Washington: US Senate Select Committee to Study Governmental Operations with Respect to Intelligence Activities, 245 pp.

Deudney, D. 1983. *Whole Earth Security: A Geopolitics of Peace*. Washington: Worldwatch Institute, Worldwatch Paper No. 55, 94 pp.

Ehrlich, A. 1984. Nuclear winter: a forecast of the climatic and biological effects of nuclear war. *Bulletin of the Atomic Scientists*, Chicago, **40**(4): 1S–15S.

Ehrlich, P. R. 1984. Nuclear winter: discovering the ecology of nuclear war. *Amicus Journal*, New York, **5**(3): 20–30.

Ehrlich, P. R. *et al.* 1983. Long-term biological consequences of nuclear war. *Science*, Washington, **222**: 1293–1300.

Falk, R. A. 1973. Environmental warfare and ecocide. *Bulletin of Peace Proposals*, Oslo, **4**: 1–17. [Also in: *Revue Belge de Droit International*, Brussels, **9**(1): 1–27.]

Falk, R. 1983. Toward a legal regime for nuclear weapons. *McGill Law Journal*, Montreal, **28**: 519–541.

Goldblat, J. 1982. *Agreements for Arms Control: A Critical Survey*. London: Taylor & Francis, 387 pp. [a SIPRI book].

Heyer, R. (ed.). 1982. *Nuclear Disarmament: Key Statements of Popes, Bishops, Councils and Churches*. New York: Paulist Press, 278 pp.

Kuper, L. 1981. *Genocide: Its Political Use in the Twentieth Century*. New Haven: Yale University Press, 256 pp.

MacBride, S., Falk, R., Asmal, K., Bercusson, B., Pradelle, G. de la and Wild, S. 1983. *Israel in Lebanon: Report of the International Commission to Enquire into Reported Violations of International Law by Israel During its Invasion of the Lebanon*. London: Ithaca Press, 282 pp.

Roberts, A. and Guelff, R. (eds). 1982. *Documents on the Laws of War*. Oxford: Clarendon Press, 498 pp.

Röling, B. V. A. and Suković, O. 1976. *Law of War and Dubious Weapons*. Stockholm: Almqvist & Wiksell, 78 pp. [a SIPRI book].

Sagan, C. 1983–84. Nuclear war and climatic catastrophe: some policy implications. *Foreign Affairs*, New York, **62**: 257–292.

Schell, J. 1984. *Abolition*. New York: Knopf, 173 pp.

Thomas, L. 1983–84. Scientific frontiers and national frontiers: a look ahead. *Foreign Affairs*, New York, **62**: 966–994.

Turco, R. P., Toon, O. B., Ackerman, T. P., Pollack, J. B. and Sagan, C. 1983. Nuclear winter: global consequences of multiple nuclear explosions. *Science*, Washington, **222**: 1283–1292.

UNGA (United Nations General Assembly). 1965. *Declarations on the Inadmissibility of Intervention in the Domestic Affairs of States and the Protection of their Independence and Sovereignty*. New York: UN General Assembly Resolution No. 2131(XX) (21 Dec 65), 2 pp.

UNGA (United Nations General Assembly). 1973a. *Effects of Atomic Radiation*. New York: UN General Assembly Resolution No. 3154(XXVIII) (14 Dec 73), 3 pp.

UNGA (United Nations General Assembly). 1973b. *Report of the United Nations Conference on the Human Environment, Stockholm, 5–16 June 1972*. New York: UN General Assembly Document No. A/CONF.48/14 Rev. 1, 77 pp.

UNGA (United Nations General Assembly). 1974a. *Prohibition of Action to Influence the Environment and Climate for Military and Other Purposes Incompatible with the*

Maintenance of International Security, Human Well-being and Health. New York: UN General Assembly Resolution No. 3264(XXIX) (9 Dec 74), 5 pp.

UNGA (United Nations General Assembly). 1974b. *Definition of Aggression*. New York: UN General Assembly Resolution No. 3314(XXIX) (14 Dec 74), 4 pp.

UNGA (United Nations General Assembly). 1982. *World Charter for Nature*. New York: UN General Assembly Resolution No. 37/7 (28 Nov 82), 5 pp.

UNWCC (United Nations War Crimes Commission). 1948. *History of the United Nations War Crimes Commission and the Development of the Laws of War*. London: His Majesty's Stationery Office, 592 pp.

Vance, C. R. 1977. United States signs convention banning environmental warfare. *Department of State Bulletin*, Washington, **76**: 633–634.

Westing, A. H. 1976. In: SIPRI (eds). *Ecological Consequences of the Second Indochina War*. Stockholm: Almqvist & Wiksell, 119 pp. + 8 pl.

Weston, B. H. 1983. Nuclear weapons versus international law: a contextual reassessment. *McGill Law Journal*, Montreal, **28**: 542–590.

5. The Environmental Modification Convention of 1977: an analysis

Jozef Goldblat
Stockholm International Peace Research Institute

I. Introduction

The Convention on the Prohibition of Military or any other Hostile Use of Environmental Modification Techniques (the Enmod Convention) resulted from several years of bilateral US–Soviet talks, as well as from multilateral negotiations held at the Geneva Conference of the Committee on Disarmament (CCD). It was signed on 18 May 1977 and entered into force on 5 October 1978.

This paper reviews the essential provisions of the Enmod Convention and of the Annex, which is an integral part of it, along with the 'Understandings' worked out at the CCD, but not written into the Convention (for the full texts of these documents, see appendix 1). The Understandings, which clarify and amplify 4 of the 10 Convention articles, form part of the *travaux préparatoires* and are important for the comprehension of the drafters' intention. The provisions analysed are those dealing with: (*a*) the subject of the prohibition; (*b*) the scope of the prohibition; (*c*) peaceful applications of environmental modification; (*d*) verification of the Convention; and (*e*) duration of the Convention. The paper concludes with some policy recommendations. It draws to some extent upon earlier studies by the author (Goldblat, 1977; 1982).

II. Subject of the prohibition

The Enmod Convention deals with changes in the environment brought about by deliberate human manipulation of natural processes, as distinct from conventional acts of warfare which might result in adverse effects on the environment. Covered by the Convention are those changes which affect the dynamics, composition or structure of the Earth, including its biota, lithosphere, hydrosphere and atmosphere, or of outer space (article II). The employment of

53

techniques producing such modifications as the means of destruction, damage or injury to another state party is prohibited. (This may be taken to mean that the use of environmental modification techniques to enhance the use of conventional weapons—for example, by dispersing fog covering airfields or other targets to be bombed—is not proscribed so long as the environmental modification technique itself produces no harm.) In the opinion of the USA, the targets alluded to include the enemy's military forces and civilian population, as well as its cities, industries, agriculture, transportation systems, communication systems and natural resources and assets (CCD, 1976a, page 14). Nor is it allowed to assist, encourage or induce other nations to engage in these activities. The threat to use the techniques in question has not been specifically forbidden, as it should have been by analogy with the provisions of the United Nations Charter dealing with the "threat or use of force" against the territorial integrity or political independence of any state (article 2, paragraph 4). One could argue, however, that the prohibition of threat is implied in the prohibition of use.

III. Scope of the prohibition

The ban under the Enmod Convention applies to the conduct of military operations during armed conflicts, as well as to hostile use (whether by military or non-military personnel) when no other weapon is being employed or when there is no overt conflict. It is applicable both to offence and defence, regardless of geographical boundaries. In the light of these explanations, which were given by the Soviet (CCD, 1976e, pages 14–20) and US (CCD, 1976e, pages 8–10) sponsors of the text, the term "hostile" alone would have sufficed as a purpose criterion upon which the Convention is based. But not all hostile uses causing harm to others are prohibited by the Convention: only those having "widespread, long-lasting or severe effects" are outlawed (article I). The meaning of these terms, according to the Understanding relating to article I, is as follows:

1. *widespread*: encompassing an area on the scale of several hundred square kilometres;[1]
2. *long-lasting*: lasting for a period of months, or approximately a season; and
3. *severe*: involving serious or significant disruption or harm to human life, natural and economic resources or other assets.

It is noted in the Understanding that the above interpretation is intended exclusively for this Convention and should not prejudice the interpretation of the same or similar terms used in connection with any other international agreement. That proviso was found necessary in order to forestall an identical interpretation

---

[1] According to the interpretation provided by the USA, the entire area would have to experience destruction, damage or injury at approximately the same time to meet the "widespread" criterion (CCD, 1976e, page 8). This could result from a single operation or it could be the cumulative result of a series of operations conducted over a period of months or years. If, over the course of several years, a total area on the scale of several hundred square kilometres were affected, but the area actually suffering destruction, damage or injury at any one time was small, the "widespread" criterion would not be met.

to be given to the terms "widespread, long-term and severe", used in the 1977 Protocol I Additional to the Geneva Conventions of 1949, and Relating to the Protection of Victims of International Armed Conflicts which was then under negotiation (for the text of the Protocol, see appendix 3). Indeed, the two documents pursue different aims. Geneva Protocol I (signed on 12 December 1977 and in force since 7 December 1978) is meant to ban the employment in armed conflict of methods or means of warfare which are intended, or may be expected, to cause serious damage to the environment, whatever the weapons used (article 55); to make this ban applicable, the presence of all three of the criteria—widespread, long term *and* severe—is required. On the other hand, the Enmod Convention forbids the use (or manipulation) of the forces of the environment as "weapons", both during hostilities and when there is no overt conflict; in this case, the presence of only one of the three criteria—widespread, long-lasting *or* severe—is enough for the environmental modification technique to be deemed outlawed.

Thus, the use of environmental modification techniques is prohibited if two requirements are met simultaneously: (*a*) that the use is hostile; and (*b*) that it causes destruction, damage or injury at, or in excess of, the threshold described above. Exempted from the prohibition are non-hostile uses of the modification techniques, even if they produce destructive effects exceeding the threshold. Equally permissible are hostile uses which produce destructive effects below the threshold. Assuming, therefore, that hostile intent has been proved (which may not be easy), it would still not be illegal, according to the Understanding, to devastate an area smaller than several hundred square kilometres, say only $100 \, km^2$ ($10000 \, ha$); or to cause adverse effects lasting for a period of weeks instead of months, or less than a season; or to bring about disruption or harm to human life, natural and economic resources or other assets, which are not "severe", "serious" or "significant", whatever these subjective terms might mean to countries of different sizes, of different population densities or at different stages of economic development. For example, Trinidad and Tobago noted that the definitions of the terms "widespread, long-lasting or severe" do not address themselves to the situation of small entities, such as the islands of the Caribbean (UNGA, 1976b, pages 22–23). Moreover, the perpetrator's perception of the gravity of such acts may not coincide with that of the victim.

However, earthquakes, tsunamis (seismic sea waves), an upset in the ecological balance of a region, changes in weather patterns (clouds, precipitation, cyclones of various types, tornadic storms), changes in climate patterns, changes in ocean currents, changes in the state of the stratospheric ozone layer and changes in the state of the ionosphere appear to be definitely prohibited by the Enmod Convention when produced by hostile use of environmental modification techniques. For it is understood that all these phenomena would result, or could reasonably be expected to result, in widespread, long-lasting or severe destruction, damage or injury (UNGA, 1976a, page 27). It has been recognized, in the Understanding relating to article II, that the use of techniques producing other phenomena could also be appropriately included,

55

insofar as the criteria of hostility and destructiveness were met. (In this connection, the USA referred to volcanic eruptions, tectonic plate movements, sea-level changes, lightning, hail and changes in the energy balance of the planet.) Nevertheless, only the most fanciful events are enumerated in the Understanding—those which are unlikely to be caused through deliberate action for warlike purposes, that is, in such a way that the effects would be felt only, or primarily, by the enemy. It is significant that long before the Enmod Convention had been negotiated, an official of the US Department of State announced that the USA was renouncing the use of climate modification techniques for hostile purposes, even if such techniques should be developed in the future (Pollack, 1972, page 20). Attempts to widen the "illustrative" list by including, for example, an upset in the hydrological balance of a region through the diversion of rivers, failed. Asked whether the use of herbicides as an instrument for upsetting the ecological balance was banned under the Enmod Convention, the US representative to the CCD stated that, in the opinion of his delegation, such use was prohibited only if the effects were widespread, long-lasting or severe (CCD, 1976e, page 10). It must be noted, however, that in the view of most nations all use of chemical methods of warfare is prohibited by international law, including the use of substances having direct toxic effects on plants (UNGA, 1969).

As a consequence of the threshold approach, the techniques which can produce more limited effects (such as precipitation modification short of changing the "weather pattern") and which are, therefore, more likely to be used to influence the environment with hostile intent in a selected area, especially in tactical military operations, have escaped proscription. As noted earlier, the use of environmental modification techniques not as direct means of destruction, damage or injury, but to facilitate the effectiveness of other weapons in producing destruction, damage or injury, also does not appear to be covered.

The narrow scope of prohibition under the Enmod Convention stands in contrast to the Soviet draft which had been submitted in 1974 (USSR, 1974). Under the latter proposal, the parties would have agreed not to use "any" means of "influencing" (not necessarily completely changing) the environment for military or any other purpose incompatible with the "maintenance of international security, human well-being and health". It is also worth noting that a study of possible international restraints on environmental warfare, prepared by the US National Security Council, and submitted to the US President in 1974, envisaged a "comprehensive" prohibition of hostile use of environmental modification techniques as one of the possible options (ACDA, 1978, page 87). The departure from the all-inclusive approach was justified by the USA with the following argument: a comprehensive ban would give rise to disputes over "trivial" issues and could create a risk of unprovable claims of violation (CCD, 1976a, pages 12–13). But what is deemed trivial by the party carrying out modification activities may not seem so to the victim. No state should have to put up with the destruction of a part of its territory, or injury to its population, whatever the scale of destruction or injury. And the high level of damage permitted under the Convention makes such acquiescence even less likely. It will be recalled that fear of "trivial" issues being raised did not prevent the conclusion, in 1972, of a convention comprehensively prohibiting biological and toxin weapons. Moreover, the imprecise and haphazard definition of the terms "widespread, long-lasting or severe" may generate controversies greater than a ban without any qualification. Thus, no convincing reason has been given as to why any hostile modification of the environment or any amount of damage caused by such modification should be tolerated at all. Even the right to use modification techniques on a state's own territory to forestall or stop foreign invasion (e.g., by opening dams or producing massive landslides) might be legitimately challenged.

Evidently, certain powers preferred not to forswear altogether the possibility of using environmental methods of warfare and to keep future options open. This conclusion can also be drawn from the fact that the Enmod Convention was conceived as a non-use agreement rather than as an arms-limitation measure. Hence, it does not prohibit the development of the prohibited techniques. In this respect, too, it is a retreat from the Soviet proposal of 1974 (USSR, 1974) under which "preparations" for use would have been expressly banned. In defence of these omissions the USA stated that research and development in the field of environmental modification have dual applicability to civilian and military ends, and are therefore impossible to verify. Again, the explanation is not convincing. Not all peaceful modification activities overlap with military ones. For example, generation of tsunamis or deliberate destruction of the ozone layer, among the phenomena specifically mentioned in the Understanding relating to article II, could hardly be envisaged for peaceful purposes.

A partial approach may have some justification in arms control agreements which restrict or forbid the possession of certain categories of weapon and leave other categories unaffected. But in agreements which prohibit the use of certain methods of warfare and thereby establish a new law of war, the notion of a threshold of damage or injury, below which the parties would retain freedom of action, seems to be incongruous. It is certainly out of place in the case of unconventional methods of warfare capable of causing mass destruction; and it is not in harmony with the humanitarian principles upon which the laws of war are based. It will be recalled that the 1925 Geneva Protocol, prohibiting the use of chemical and bacteriological weapons, makes no distinction between quantitatively more or less severe effects caused by these weapons. It is true that there have been disputes regarding the applicability of the prohibition to a few types of chemical agent, mainly tear gas and herbicides. However, it has never been suggested that allowance should be made for some degree of harm to human life with the use of weapons which are indisputably covered by the Protocol, as in the case of the Enmod Convention.

The protection from hostile uses of environmental modification techniques extends only to parties (article I), that is, to states which have ratified or acceded to the Convention (article IX). The negotiators were of the view that if non-parties were also covered by such a protection, there would be no incentive for them to assume contractual obligations.

IV. Peaceful applications of environmental modification

A review of possible environmental modification techniques shows that a number of them have peaceful applications. Thus, fog or cloud dispersion could be applied at civilian airports, seaports or other major civilian enterprises that are thus inhibited. Conversely, fog or cloud generation could be useful to limit heat loss from crops subject to frost damage. Suppression of conditions that lead to hailstone precipitation could help to reduce damage to crops. Manipulation of storms could be used to moderate the intensity of hurricanes, or to disperse or redirect them. Rain making could be employed for the relief of drought or for extinguishing forest fires. Stimulation of weak earthquakes could be applied to relieve stress conditions that otherwise might lead to destructive natural earthquakes. Moreover, forest burning is used to relieve conditions that lead to uncontrolled fires. Precipitating a snow avalanche is used for controlled avalanche release. And river diversion is commonly used for irrigation, for navigation or for power-generating purposes.

The incentive to develop these techniques is great and the Enmod Convention stipulates that their use shall not be hindered. This does not mean that there are no restrictions on such use. Indeed, the relevant clause (article III, paragraph 1) contains a proviso to the effect that the use of modification techniques for peaceful purposes shall be without prejudice to "generally recognized principles and applicable rules of international law concerning such use". But the Understanding relating to article III makes it clear that the Convention does not deal with the question of whether or not a given use of environmental modification techniques for peaceful purposes is in accordance with generally recognized principles and applicable rules of international law. Thus, the legal grounds for complaints about breaches of this clause have been left undetermined.

A more general question is involved here, namely, whether, and if so to what extent, a state incurs international responsibility when it causes injury or damage outside its territory. A number of treaties have been concluded in recent times that establish the liability of states for acts producing harmful extra-territorial effects, particularly in connection with peaceful uses of nuclear energy, exploration of space or sea transportation. In a few cases, in the absence of codified law, the principle of liability has been accepted *de facto*. For example, the USA paid compensation in the case of the *Lucky Dragon*, a Japanese tuna trawler, in which Japanese nationals suffered a fatality, injuries and material losses as a result of the radioactive fallout from a US nuclear explosion at Bikini atoll in 1954. The USA also paid compensation for the damages caused to crops and fields by the hydrogen bombs which accidentally fell from a US bomber to the ground and scattered their radioactive contents at Palomares, Spain, in 1966. However, some injuries may not be readily measured and compensated for.

Principles specifically related to the environment are included in the Declaration of the United Nations Conference on the Human Environment of 1972 (UNGA, 1973). According to principle 21 of the Declaration, nations have the responsibility "to ensure that activities within their jurisdiction or control do not cause damage to the environment of other States or of areas beyond the limits of national jurisdiction" (UNGA, 1973, page 5). A passing reference to the Declaration has been made in the preamble to the Enmod Convention, but it is not clear whether it reflects concern about the preservation of the environment in general, or acceptance of the applicability of the Declaration to the Convention. In any event, the binding force of the Declaration is questionable. International environmental law will have to regulate the question of responsibility for harm resulting from legitimate environmental modification activities for peaceful purposes. A convention prohibiting hostile applications does not need to deal with peaceful applications, although perhaps in the last analysis, the injury suffered matters more than the stated intention of the country causing it.

The parties to the Enmod Convention undertake to facilitate and participate in the "fullest possible" exchange of scientific and technological information on the use of environmental modification techniques for peaceful purposes. They shall contribute, as far as they are "in a position to do so", to international economic and scientific co-operation in the preservation, improvement and peaceful utilization of the environment, with due consideration for the needs of the developing areas of the world (article III, paragraph 2). These pledges have so far proved to be of no consequence.

V. Verification of the Convention

The parties have undertaken to prohibit and prevent any activity in violation of the provisions of the Enmod Convention (article IV). However, to verify the observance of a ban on hostile manipulation of the environment is a considerably more difficult task than to verify compliance with an undertaking not to use a specific, traditional weapon (see also Krass, chapter 6). Indeed, certain hostile modification activities could perhaps be carried out in such a way that the affected country would not be aware for quite a long time, if ever, that it was under attack. But, should there be suspicions, the following questions would inevitably arise before a charge of violation could be made: (a) whether changes in the environment which had harmed a particular country were the result of human activities in another country or simply natural fluctuations (which can be very wide); (b) whether the effects produced were widespread, long-lasting or severe; and (c) whether the damage was caused deliberately, with hostile intent, or was just an accidental consequence of peaceful (or even military but non-hostile) uses of modification techniques. To clarify these and other problems relating to the objectives of the Convention and to its application, the parties may resort to consultations (article V). These consultations could be carried out either on a bilateral basis, or through "appropriate" international procedures. The latter may include the services of international organizations, both intergovernmental (e.g., the World Meteorological Organization or United Nations Environment Programme) and non-governmental (such as international scientific unions), as well as a Consultative Committee of Experts to be convened by the depositary of the Convention (the United Nations Secretary-General) upon request submitted by a party (article V). The functions and rules of procedure of the Consultative Committee, to which any party may appoint an expert, are set out in the Annex to the Convention, which constitutes an integral part of it. The role of the Committee is restricted to fact-finding and to providing expert views on problems raised by the party requesting its services. The experts will have the right, through the depositary of the Convention (or his or her representative) serving as the chairperson of the Committee, to request from states and from international organizations such information and assistance as would be considered desirable for the accomplishment of their work. No voting on matters of substance will be allowed, but a summary of the findings, incorporating all views and information presented to the Committee during its proceedings, would be distributed to the parties.

The Consultative Committee, as a body, is not entitled to pass judgement on whether a violation has occurred or who has committed it, or to formulate recommendations. The political decision that a party has been harmed or "is likely to be harmed" as a result of a violation of the Enmod Convention, including the determination of culpability, will be the prerogative of the United Nations Security Council. Each party may lodge a complaint with the Security Council, either directly or after first making use of the consultation machinery. In the latter event, the complainant could benefit from the evidence already collected to support the validity of the charge. However, the Security Council may initiate its own investigation of the allegations in co-operation with the parties.

Although its functions within the framework of the complaints procedure are strictly circumscribed, the Consultative Committee has been given a role in the verification process which is not negligible.[2] The right to decide procedural questions relative to the organization of its work, by a majority of those present and voting, enables the Committee to order an inquiry. The fact that there will be no voting on questions other than procedural ones is, no doubt, a shortcoming. But this shortcoming is not irreparable, if the findings are drafted in such a way as to make the prevailing opinion easily discernible. The essential point is that experts will be given an opportunity to examine the particulars of each case before a complaint reaches the level of political action, and to make their views widely known. It would then be up to the complaining country to draw its own conclusions from the information received and decide upon further action: it may either drop the charges or bring the matter before the United Nations Security Council, asking it formally to condemn the violator.

The United Nations Security Council would act "in accordance with the provisions of the Charter of the United Nations" (article V, paragraph 2) as it is, in any case, already bound to act in all instances regarding "threats to peace, breaches of the peace, and acts of aggression" (UN Charter, chapter VII), irrespective of whether or not a specific treaty has been violated. Security Council

---

[2] According to a proposal put forward by the Netherlands at the CCD (but not accepted by the Committee), the consultative body would be a standing organ, not a committee constituted *ad hoc*; it would not only provide an expert view on phenomena which have a bearing on the application of the Enmod Convention, but would also have the right to initiate an inquiry into relevant facts and, in addition, consider proposals for improving the viability of the Convention, including recommendations for amendments (CCD, 1976b, pages 33–35).

decisions on substantive matters are made by an affirmative vote of 9 of the 15 members of the Council, with no permanent member voting negatively. Thereby China, France, the United Kingdom, the USA and the USSR, the permanent members of the Council, have the power of veto. The great-power veto has been seen to be used to block not only substantive decisions but also proposals for the establishment of organs for investigation or observation. A suggestion made by Sweden that, in initiating an investigation, the permanent members of the Security Council should give up their right of veto, was not accepted (CCD, 1976c, pages 25–26). A complainant may find it unacceptable that the inequality of states under the United Nations Charter, whatever its historical justification, should be carried over to relations under other international instruments. Moreover, certain members (permanent or non-permanent) of the Security Council, called upon to examine a charge of violation of the Convention, may not themselves be party to that Convention.[3] It could be inconvenient to seek redress from such a body. In view of these uncertainties, an injured country may decide to forgo the recourse to the Security Council and instead pursue another course of action on the basis of the findings of the Consultative Committee, if it considers the findings to be sufficient proof of violation.

VI. Duration of the Convention

Unlike some other arms control treaties, the Enmod Convention has no withdrawal clause and formally is of unlimited duration (article VII). (Under a withdrawal clause, each party reserves the right to withdraw from the treaty if it decides that extraordinary events, related to the subject matter of the treaty, have jeopardized its supreme interests.) However, according to the 1969 Vienna Convention on the Law of Treaties, material breach of a multilateral treaty (i.e., violation of a provision essential to the accomplishment of the object or purpose of the treaty) by one of the parties entitles the other parties by unanimous agreement to suspend the operations of the treaty or to terminate it, either in the relations between themselves and the defaulting state or among all the parties; it also entitles a party specially affected by the breach to invoke it as a ground for suspending the operation of the treaty in the relations between itself and the defaulting state (Vienna Convention, article 60.2[b]). If a multilateral treaty is of such a character that a material breach of its provisions by one party radically changes the position of every party with respect to the further performance of its obligations under the treaty, any party is entitled to invoke the breach as a ground for suspending the operation of the treaty with respect to itself (Vienna Convention, article 60.2[c]). It is not certain whether a convention prohibiting the use of environmental modification techniques for hostile purposes should be considered as belonging to this category. Were this the case, a material breach of

[3] China refused to participate in the vote on the United Nations General Assembly resolution dealing with the Enmod Convention, stating that the Convention was designed to divert attention from "immediate concerns" (UNGA, 1976b, page 41). France abstained, explaining that the text of the Convention may give rise to technical, legal and political difficulties (UNGA, 1976b, pages 51–52). Neither country had joined the Convention as of April 1984.

the Enmod Convention would give any party the right to free itself from the assumed obligations. The absence of a withdrawal clause would not restrict that right.

VII. Conclusion

Generally speaking, constraints on new weapons before they have been fully developed, and especially on techniques of warfare which are inherently indiscriminate and unpredictable in their effects, could, as preventive measures, contribute to the circumscription of the arms race. This applies to the harnessing of environmental forces as weapons of war, even though very few environmental modification techniques having significant military utility have as yet been identified (see Westing, chapter 1). But to be effective, the constraints must be unambiguous, as nearly all-inclusive as possible and without any loopholes. The Enmod Convention is far from meeting these requirements. It is not clear what is actually banned by the Convention, nor is it clear how hostile intent can be adequately established. Moreover, the Convention is a half-measure, for it prohibits only those techniques which are covered by other treaties, or do not exist, or are the subject of scientific speculation, or which, if proved feasible, could hardly be used as rational weapons of war. The Convention thus appears to condone hostile manipulation of the environment with some unspecified "benign" means. It is also deficient in that it bans only hostile use, but not the development or possession of modification techniques for such use. No wonder that five years after its entry into force, the Enmod Convention could claim no more than 43 parties, including only three of the five permanent members of the United Nations Security Council (see appendix 2, section II). To become a meaningful contribution to the cause of halting the arms race—which is one of the main purposes proclaimed in the preamble—and to attract new parties, the Convention would have to be substantially amended.

In the first place, the prohibition of the environmental modification techniques should be made comprehensive. Comprehensiveness could be achieved by removing the threshold established by the Enmod Convention, which limits the ban to uses having only "widespread, long-lasting or severe effects". In other words, the Convention should be made applicable to *any* hostile use of the techniques in question. This could reduce the apprehensions of a number of countries about the intentions of the major military powers.

Second, the parties should undertake to abstain not only from hostile use of environmental modification techniques, but also from preparations for such use. This implies constraints on militarily oriented development of the techniques. Verification of compliance would be facilitated if all research and development in the environmental field were placed under civilian control. Activities unencumbered by military secrecy would be more accessible to supervision. Consequently, states could assume an obligation to give advance notification of all major experiments in environmental modification and subject them to international observation in order to demonstrate that their purposes were genuinely peaceful. Large-scale internationalization of research and development in the field of peaceful uses of environmental modification techniques could, apart from obvious scientific, economic and technological advantages, provide additional assurance that substantial resources were not diverted to hostile military ends.

Third, it would be desirable to prohibit the hostile use of modification techniques against *any* state or people, instead of confining the ban, as the Enmod Convention does, to injuries to parties, for an environmental weapon would strike both combatants and non-combatants in an indiscriminate way in contravention of the basic rule of international law requiring protection of the civilian population. Another justification for such an absolute prohibition is the difficulty, if not the impossibility, of circumscribing the effects of the use of an environmental modification technique within definite geographic boundaries so as to injure a non-party without injuring a party. These considerations certainly carry more weight than the argument that an obligation *erga omnes* would remove an incentive for states to join the Convention.

According to article VI of the Enmod Convention, any party may propose amendments by submitting the proposed text to the depositary. The amendments will enter into force for all parties which have accepted them, upon the deposit of instruments of acceptance by a majority. It is the understanding of the parties (Understanding relating to article VIII) that a proposal to amend the Convention may also be considered at conferences periodically convened to review the operation of the Convention and to examine the effectiveness of its provisions in eliminating the dangers of any hostile use of environmental modification techniques.

The deletion of the threshold limitation on the scope of the environmental modification ban is of capital importance. It will be recalled that of the two main sponsors of the Enmod Convention, the USSR had all along advocated a total prohibition. The USA opposed comprehensiveness during the negotiations, but subsequently the US Secretary of State indicated that the USA would be ready to re-examine the threshold issue (Vance, 1977). As regards restrictions on development, again there appears to be no insurmountable obstacle, for the Soviet delegation had also been insisting on such restriction in negotiating the Convention at the CCD, and the US Senate, even before the intergovernmental negotiations began, favoured the cessation of "any research or experimentation directed to the development" of any environmental or geophysical modification activity (defined to include weather, climate, earthquake and ocean modification) as a "weapon of war" (Senate, 1973, page 3). A refusal by the great powers to bring about these changes, which would not even significantly restrict their practical military options, would cast doubt on their willingness to make significant advances in the field of arms control.

References

ACDA (US Arms Control and Disarmament Agency). 1978. *Environmental Assessment for the Convention on the Prohibition of Military or any Other Hostile Use of Environmental Modification Techniques.* Washington: US Arms Control & Disarmament Agency. [Reprinted in: Pell, C. (ed.). 1978. *Environmental Modification Treaty* (Hearings, 3 Oct 78). Washington: US Senate Committee on Foreign Relations, 127 pp.: pp. 87–127.]

CCD (Conference of the Committee on Disarmament). 1976a. *Final Record of the Six Hundred and Ninety-First Meeting.* Geneva: Conference of the Committee on Disarmament Document No. CCD/PV.691 (4 Mar 76), 17 pp.

CCD (Conference of the Committee on Disarmament). 1976b. *Final Record of the Six Hundred and Ninety-Second Meeting.* Geneva: Conference of the Committee on Disarmament Document No. CCD/PV.692 (9 Mar 76), 36 pp.

CCD (Conference of the Committee on Disarmament). 1976c. *Final Record of the Six Hundred and Ninety-Seventh Meeting.* Geneva: Conference of the Committee on Disarmament Document No. CCD/PV.697 (25 Mar 76), 32 pp.

CCD (Conference of the Committee on Disarmament). 1976d. *Final Record of the Six Hundred and Nineth-Eighth Meeting.* Geneva: Conference of the Committee on Disarmament Document No. CCD/PV.698 (30 Mar 76), 20 pp.

CCD (Conference of the Committee on Disarmament). 1976e. *Final Record of the Seven Hundred and Third Meeting.* Geneva: Conference of the Committee on Disarmament Document No. CCD/PV.703 (20 Apr 76), 20 pp.

Goldblat, J. 1977. Environmental warfare convention: how meaningful is it? *Ambio*, Stockholm, **6**: 216–221.

Goldblat, J. 1982. ENMOD convention. In: Goldblat, J. (ed.). *Agreements for Arms Control: A Critical Survey.* London: Taylor & Francis, 387 pp.: pp. 51–53, 228–231, 303–335. [a SIPRI book].

Pollack, H. 1972. Statement of Herman Pollack, Director, Bureau of International Scientific and Technological Affairs, Department of State. In: Pell, C. (ed.). *Prohibiting Military Weather Modification* (Hearings, 26 and 27 Jul 72). Washington: US Senate Committee on Foreign Relations, 162 pp.: pp. 17–29.

Senate, US. 1973. *Resolution Expressing the Sense of the Senate that the United States Government Should Seek the Agreement of Other Governments to a Proposed Treaty Prohibiting the Use of Any Environmental or Geophysical Modification Activity as a Weapon of War, or the Carrying Out of Any Research or Experimentation Directed Thereto.* Washington: US Senate (93rd Congress) Resolution No. 71 (11 Jul 73), 6 pp.

UNGA (United Nations General Assembly). 1969. *Question of Chemical and Bacteriological (Biological) Weapons.* New York: UN General Assembly Resolution No. 2603A(XXIV) (16 Dec 69), 5 pp.

UNGA (United Nations General Assembly). 1973. *Report of the United Nations Conference on the Human Environment, Stockholm, 5–16 June 1972.* New York: UN General Assembly Document No. A/CONF.48/14/Rev.1, 77 pp.

UNGA (United Nations General Assembly). 1976a. *Verbatim Record of the 20th Meeting [of the First Committee].* New York: UN General Assembly Document No. A/C.1/31/PV.20 (2 Nov 76), 77 pp.

UNGA (United Nations General Assembly). 1976b. *Verbatim Record of the 51st Meeting [of the First Committee].* New York: UN General Assembly Document No. A/C.1/31/PV.51 (3 Dec 76), 66 pp.

USSR (Union of Soviet Socialist Republics). 1974. *Draft Convention on the Prohibition of Action to Influence the Environment and Climate for Military and Other Purposes Incompatible with the Maintenance of International Security, Human Well-being and Health.* New York: UN General Assembly Document No. A/C.1/L.675/Rev.1 (21 Nov 74), 2 + 5 pp.: Annex (5 pp.).

Vance, C. R. 1977. United States signs convention banning environmental warfare. *Department of State Bulletin*, Washington, **76**: 633–634.

6. The Environmental Modification Convention of 1977: the question of verification

Allan S. Krass

Hampshire College, Amherst, Massachusetts[1]

I. Introduction

The Convention on the Prohibition of Military or any other Hostile Use of Environmental Modification Techniques (the Enmod Convention) was signed in May 1977 and entered into force in October 1978 (for the text of the Convention, see appendix 2, section I). Now in 1984, with the Convention's first review conference in September, it has the rare distinction among treaties of its type of having no outstanding accusations of non-compliance sullying its record. This allows an approach to the sensitive problem of adequate verification of the Convention without the added burden of a political atmosphere highly charged with suspicion and recrimination.

The problem of verification and the advent of a review conference have an intimate historical connection. Concerns about verification caused (or rationalized) the US insistence on the so-called threshold provision which limits violations to those activities which cause "widespread, long-lasting or severe" effects (ACDA, 1978, page 96). And it was this same threshold provision that led a number of other states to demand periodic reviews of the Convention with the rather ill-concealed purpose of repealing the threshold provision as soon as possible. As one analyst has put it, "The demand for review conferences grew in direct proportion to American insistence on retention of the threshold wording in article I" (Juda, 1978, page 984).

It is therefore highly appropriate to re-evaluate the problem of verification of the Enmod Convention, both in a general way and with respect to the threshold and other specific provisons. Verification has become a more central feature of the arms control debate than it was during the Enmod Convention negotiations in the mid-1970s, and the Convention must be reconsidered in the light of this growing centrality of verification concerns. It can be argued with considerable

[1] At the time of his participation in this project the author was on sabbatical leave from his institution, working at SIPRI.

justification that verification issues have, in fact, become excessively prominent in arms control negotiations. But however one might wish for a more balanced and realistic approach, there is no avoiding the fact that verification has become a major public concern, at least in the USA and some other Western nations. Since public opinion in these states is a crucial variable relating to any future progress in arms control, there is no alternative to making the effort to deal carefully and rigorously with verification issues.

This chapter begins with a brief review of those provisions of the Enmod Convention which require verification, and the mechanisms established in the Convention for verifying them. It goes on to apply the general principles of verification to possible extensions of the Convention and concludes that there are some potentially significant modifications which can be made without undue sacrifice of verifiability.

II.   The present Enmod Convention

The activities proscribed by the Enmod Convention are specifically limited to "military or any other hostile use of environmental modification techniques having widespread, long-lasting or severe effects" (article I.1). It is also forbidden to "assist, encourage or induce" other states to engage in such activities (article I.2). From the point of view of verification this second prohibition would seem to present serious difficulties in either monitoring compliance or demonstrating non-compliance, and there is no mechanism specified in the Convention which seems appropriate for monitoring this provision. For this reason article I.2 will not be dealt with in this chapter, nor will the problem of establishing hostile intent (see article II). Thus, attention will be focused entirely on the technical violations specified in article I.1.

Verification of the Enmod Convention is to be carried out by both national technical means and certain international means specified in article V. National technical means are not mentioned specifically in this Convention as they are, for example, in the two SALT (Strategic Arms Limitation Talks) agreements and the Partial Nuclear Test Ban Treaty of 1963 (Goldblat, 1982), but they are nevertheless implicit, since it is clear that any state will use whatever means it has at its disposal to determine the causes and assess the effects of any damaging environmental modifications it may suffer. Such efforts would inevitably precede any decision by the state to request an investigation by an international Consultative Committee of Experts or to lodge a complaint with the United Nations Security Council, the two mechanisms specified in the Convention for dealing with alleged violations.

The key verification mechanism of the Enmod Convention is the Consultative Committee of Experts which is to be convened by the United Nations Secretary-General (the depositary) at the request of any party to the Convention. This Committee is strictly limited to making "appropriate findings of fact" and is prohibited from "voting on matters of substance" (Convention annexes 1 and 2). If the Committee is limited to establishing facts, then its actual role in verification can include a determination of whether an environmental modification in fact occurred and what kind of technique was used, as well as a judgement on whether or not the effects of the modification were "widespread" or "long-lasting". Both of these criteria are defined in quantitative terms in the Understandings relating to the Convention, a document drafted by the Conference of the Committee on Disarmament (CCD), but not formally a part of it (for the text of the Understandings, see appendix 2, section III). In the Understanding relating to article I, 'widespread' is defined as "on the scale of several hundred square kilometres", and 'long-lasting' is defined as "a period of months, or approximately a season". Although some ambiguity still remains in these definitions they are clear enough to allow "factual" conclusions as to whether or not they were exceeded, assuming of course that the investigation is carried out in timely fashion, the scientific phenomena are well enough understood, and the data are adequate to allow a thorough analysis.

On the other hand, the question of whether the effects were "severe" is in essence a subjective judgement (hence a matter of substance) and not amenable to quantitative definition (as would be a fact). The attempt made to define this criterion in the Understanding relating to article I is linguistically circular and in no sense quantitative. The definition boils down to the use of the synonyms "serious or significant". One analyst who has struggled with this problem attempted to resolve it with the word "importance" (Wunsch, 1980). In his opinion this solves the problem because "The consultative committee of experts can make the determination whether the disruptive activity is important to the injured state" (Wunsch, 1980, page 124). It is true that the Consultative Committee could establish certain quantitative relationships between the damage done and the economic and human assets of the state involved (e.g., a fraction of population displaced or a percentage of agricultural production lost), but neither the Convention nor the Understandings gives a specific threshold in these terms, so the question of importance (or severity or seriousness or significance) cannot be decided on factual grounds. Since the level of severity cannot be a finding of fact, the decision on this criterion could not be made in the Consultative Committee, but would have to be made in the United Nations Security Council itself. It is worth emphasizing, however, that the threshold consists of any one of the three criteria, not all three together. Therefore, a factual finding that an effect was "long-lasting", whether or not it was widespread or severe, could establish a *prima facie* case for a violation.

These general comments are about all that can be made about the verification provisions without focusing on the specifics of potential violations. For this purpose it is essential to have some sense of the relative likelihood and importance of various efforts to modify the environment for hostile purposes. Otherwise one is required to classify and analyse all sorts of bizarre scenarios. There has been much too great a tendency in past analyses of the problem to treat fantastic and militarily implausible activities as if they were genuine threats as weapons. Such things as decoupling or melting of the polar ice caps with nuclear weapons (presumably by those "landlocked equatorial countries" which would "stand to benefit" from an inundation of the world's coastal areas), and introducing low-frequency electro-magnetic oscillations into the atmosphere with "carefully timed, artificially-excited [lightning] strokes" were treated as serious possibilities by one scientist (MacDonald, 1968). Earlier, a US military writer had been alarmed to discover that "Many Soviet weather problems could be solved through arctic melt accomplished by . . . the launching of a satellite carrying a thermonuclear reactor [which] would be put into a highly elliptical orbit that would approach the earth only in the vicinity of the North Pole" (Kotsch, 1960, page 78). A more recent example of this genre is the suggestion that the orbit of an asteroid might be altered in order to make the asteroid strike the Earth in "some strategic region" such as a missile complex (Sullivan, 1983, page C8).

There is another very popular scenario which also deserves to be laid to rest. In this fantasy, one state "systematically and covertly" dissipates part or all of the clouds over its own territory in order to deprive a neighbouring state of rain and "reduce it to a semi-desert over a period of time" (Kotsch, 1960, page 76). The idea that such a programme is both technically feasible and capable of being carried out in total secrecy for several years is utterly unrealistic, yet it has re-appeared often in analyses of the environmental modification problem. None of the analysts who mentions it makes any attempt to study the scenario in detail or to assess its real military utility. It is simply proposed as the sort of thing that might happen unless there exists an appropriate treaty or an appropriate deterrent. A more detailed analysis of the secret weather war scenario is provided in annex 6.1.

These comments are not intended to dismiss completely either the possibility of irrational or bizarre behaviour by insane or desperate leaders or the danger of covert operations by one state against the population or resources of another. But there is little point in considering insane or desperate acts in the context of a discussion of treaties, since such legal instruments would have little or no effect on the actions of states led by madness or driven to the point where their national survival is at stake. Treaties can only operate in a climate of rationality in which the mutual benefits of certain kinds of restraint remain apparent to all parties even in time of hostilities.

Threats of covert hostile operations in times of peace are indeed serious, and some of these could involve environmental modifications. One example might be the release of an insect or disease for which there is no control in order to destroy the crops of an unsuspecting state. Such an attack, if successful, could be virtually impossible to attribute to another state or even to identify as a hostile act. But it is not at all clear that such an attack falls within the purview of the Enmod Convention, that is, whether it represents a "deliberate manipulation of natural processes"; and such acts may well be already prohibited by other treaties. If we focus on those environmental manipulations referred to in article II of the Convention and the Understanding relating to it, then it is difficult to see how any of these activities could be both effective and covert. Indeed, one might hypothesize an inverse relationship between the effectiveness of an environmental modification technique and its capability for successful covert application. It would be a useful exercise to attempt to uncover any counter-examples to this hypothesis. The analysis of the attached secret weather war scenario (annex 6.1) might serve as a model of how to approach such questions. Meanwhile it does little good, and possibly much harm, to continue postulating scenarios which have little relevance to rational military or political objectives.

The real danger inherent in a disregard for responsible standards of analysis is that it can create a climate or irrational fear and suspicion among states. Indeed, "The greatest threat to peace from weather warfare may come not from the actual employment of the techniques but from the fears and perceptions which states develop about what others could be doing to them by these means" (Weiss, 1975, page 65). It should also be noted that this use of unlikely or impossible scenarios of clandestine cheating is not confined to considerations of the Enmod Convention. It has become the stock-in-trade of many who wish to undermine all public confidence in arms control.

A far more sensible approach to an assessment of the real threat of hostile environmental modifications would be to use the criteria of technical feasibility, danger to the environment, and military utility in order to reduce the number of plausible violation scenarios. In one such effort, the Swedish delegation to the CCD reduced a Canadian delegation list of 19 possible techniques (Canada, 1975) to the 5 "least questionable" ones (Sweden, 1975): (a) steering storms; (b) making snow avalanches and landslides; (c) modifying permafrost areas; (d) diverting and polluting rivers and destroying dams; and (e) making rain or snow. Even some of these were of questionable significance according to the Swedish assessment.

All of this is relevant to the question of verification because in order to assess the verifiability of the Enmod Convention one must have some idea of the range of activities that must be monitored and evaluated. If a volcano erupts somewhere or an asteroid collides with the Earth in a "strategic location", must a Consultative Committee of Experts be convened to determine whether the event is of covert hostile origin? Does one have to reach a conclusion on how difficult or easy such investigations would be in order to form a judgement on the verifiability of the Convention? Such exercises, however technically intriguing, have little relevance to the real world of military threats to the environment.

The problem becomes manageable if one concentrates on those activities which were the major reason behind the desire for consummating an Enmod Convention in the first place: the rain-making and herbicide (forest and crop destruction) operations carried out by the USA during the Second Indochina War. These activities remain probably the most serious environmental modification threats for actual use in warfare, yet it is interesting to note that the use of herbicides for vegetation destruction is not included in the above-mentioned Canadian list of environmental warfare techniques. This may be a reflection of the belief of that delegation that such activities were already prohibited under existing treaties.

Another class of environmental modification threat which is very real and very serious is the targeting of installations such as nuclear reactors, radioactive waste disposal sites and offshore oil rigs in warfare (Westing, chapter 1). Although such activities could certainly create widespread, long-lasting and severe effects, it is not clear whether they can really be considered environmental modification techniques in the terms of the Enmod Convention.

Once its scope is narrowed down to the small set of militarily and techno-logically realistic environmental modification techniques, the present Enmod Convention seems to present no serious problem of verifiability. Because of the threshold provision, violations are limited to relatively large operations (unless smaller-scale operations can be demonstrated to have "severe" effects), so the sensitivity of detection of these activities does not have to be very great in order to detect violations. However, problems of verification would begin to arise if extensions of the Convention beyond its present limited scope were considered. Such problems are the subject of the next section.

III. Possible amendments to the Enmod Convention

The process of verification can be broken down into several stages, each of which involves higher degrees of technical and political judgement than the previous one. The first stage, the most straightforward of the processes, is usually called 'monitoring' and is simply the gathering of data. Judgement enters here in deciding which kinds of data are to be gathered and what levels of precision, sensitivity and comprehensiveness are necessary for the task to be accomplished. The second stage is 'analysis', in which the data are processed according to estab-lished procedures in order to reveal objects or activities of interest. In the third stage, 'identification', such objects or activities are judged either to have been detected or not detected at some level of confidence. If the identification is positive then the significance of the violation must be assessed in the fourth stage, a process of 'evaluation'. In the final stage a judgement must be made as to the appropriate 'response'.

It is clear from the wording of the Enmod Convention that the drafters had in mind confining the role of the Consultative Committee of Experts to the first three stages (monitoring, analysis and identification) and assigning the last two (evaluation and response) to the United Nations Security Council. This division of labour seems both appropriate and inevitable given the political sensitivity of the evaluation and response stages. It also clarifies the two major obstacles to effective application of the Convention should an accusation of non-compliance arise: (a) the question of on-site inspection; and (b) the possible use of the veto power enjoyed by the five permanent members of the Security Council to terminate the verification process.

The monitoring function is the first essential step in the verification process, but given the nature of the violations which can be anticipated and the wording of article V of the Enmod Convention, this function cannot be of a continuous nature as is, say, the monitoring of missile sites by satellites or nuclear explosions by seismographs. It will, instead, be of an *ad hoc* nature, requiring timely and extended access to the affected area as well as possibly to areas from which the modification was or is being controlled. This raises the problem of on-site inspection, a traditional bone of contention in arms control negotiations.

If it were proposed to extend the Enmod Convention by prohibiting the use of environmental modification techniques by a state against its own people on its own territory, the need for on-site inspection would be a serious obstacle to approval of this extension. Another possibility is the use of environmental warfare techniques by one state on the territory of an 'ally', in which case the use may not be regarded as hostile and no complaint would be filed. But in the case where the attacked state does perceive a hostile intent and does file a complaint there would seem to be no difficulty in permitting a Consultative Committee of Experts to examine the affected area on the territory of the affected state. The recent co-operation of the Iranian government in facilitating the investigation by a United Nations team of experts of alleged Iraqi chemical-weapon attacks provides an excellent example of the sort of behaviour to be expected should there be an accusation of an environmental modification attack (Andersson *et al.*, 1984).

Monitoring the *source* of an alleged environmental modification attack—if it is remote from the affected area—is another matter. Some possibly important portions of such monitoring might be carried out by remote sensing agents such as satellites, radars, communication intercepts and seismographs. If the Consultative Committee of Experts were allowed access to data from such sources much might be learned. Unfortunately, all such sources are currently under the control of sovereign states, and many of them are considered among the most highly secret of military assets. Access to data from most of these sources by an international team of experts is therefore doubtful unless a state possessing such capabilities has a political interest in contributing evidence. However, such evidence would be likely to be highly controversial once the complaint reached the United Nations Security Council, so even if it were obtainable it would be of dubious value.

The problem of access to data from highly sophisticated remote-sensing devices seems to recur frequently in international treaties and has, for example, already been identified in the Seabed Treaty of 1971, which forbids the placing of weapons of mass destruction on the ocean floor. The problem has been well stated by Dore (1982, page 25):

Because only the two major powers possess the technology for meaningful verification, and since only these two powers claim to perceive the sort of worldwide interests which might lead to the emplacement of weapons of mass destruction on the seabed, the process of consultation envisaged by Article III [of the 1971 Seabed Treaty] is reduced to consultation between a less-developed party and one superpower in opposition to the other superpower.

To the extent that a given environmental modification technique involves sophisticated or massive technological capabilities and can be executed at a substantial distance from the affected area, a similar problem could be expected to arise in verifying the Enmod Convention. Fortunately, however, it is at present possible to eliminate virtually all such techniques as highly impractical and improbable. There appears to remain only a small group of techniques, all of which are relatively unsophisticated technically and must be executed at or very near the affected area. This would seem to remove most of the obstacles to the effective inspection required for adequate verification as long as other criteria such as timeliness and adequate personnel and equipment were met by the inspection team.

The other major problem lies with the United Nations Security Council where evaluations must be made and responses decided. Any of the permanent members can use the veto power at this stage to prevent decisions and actions. It is an interesting historical fact that the first serious proposal to suspend the veto power in the Security Council was in the context of a problem of verification and response: the so-called Baruch Plan for the international control of atomic energy (Goldblat, 1982, page 13). Suggestions to limit the veto power are still being made (CCD, 1976, pages 25–26; Wunsch, 1980, page 131), but they seem as unlikely to succeed now as they did in 1946. Any restriction of the veto power would set an historic precedent, and the Enmod Convention hardly provides the sort of issue on which one would expect such a major breakthrough.

These technical and political constraints define the context in which proposed extensions of the Enmod Convention must be discussed. The first possible extension is the removal of the "widespread, long-lasting or severe" threshold. A second might be the specification of certain environmental modification techniques whose use is prohibited at any level of damage. A third set of extensions might seek to add to article I the development, production and/or possession of environmental modification technologies, which now prohibits only their use. A fourth possible extension would be to make the Consultative Committee of Experts a permanent standing body and give it the authority and capability to carry out continuous monitoring and analysis activities.

The abolition of the threshold without any other change in the Enmod Convention would reduce the clarity and specificity of some phases of the verification process. Although the threshold in the present Convention has the weakness of permitting objectionable activities at low levels of damage, it has the virtue of confining the monitoring process to large, clearly identifiable manipulations of the environment, thereby placing full emphasis on the effects of the manipulation rather than on the techniques employed to achieve it. In fact, no technique is mentioned explicitly in the Convention; there is only an illustrative, explicitly non-comprehensive, list of examples given in the Understanding relating to article II (for the text of the Understandings, see appendix 2, section III). As has already been noted, these Understandings are not part of the Convention itself.

One possible way to shift the emphasis in the Enmod Convention from effects to techniques would be to add a precise listing of prohibited environmental modification techniques. The problem with such specific lists is well known: everything that is not specifically prohibited must be assumed to be permitted. This is a real problem, but its seriousness must be measured in relation to the alternative problem presented by the existence of a threshold which permits the application of any technique as long as its effects do not exceed certain more or less well-defined limits. One cannot make a generalization as to which type of treaty is easier to verify. In fact, if forest destruction attacks are considered there would seem to be no verification problem at almost any level of effect, and a total prohibition should be verifiable. For rain making the situation is different (at least based on the experience in Indochina), and small-scale rain-making efforts might be difficult to detect or identify. But here again the issue of military utility comes to the fore, and one can ask whether there is in fact any use at all for small-scale rain making in combat: the experience of the Second Indochina War seems to have demonstrated that it is very little (Westing, 1977, pages 55–57).

A third variation on this theme would be to give up the threshold and continue to leave the prohibited techniques unspecified. Under such a treaty the complaint and investigation procedures would be the same, and the Consultative Committee of Experts could still establish whatever matters of fact were accessible to it (via monitoring and analysis). But without any quantitative threshold or list of prohibited activities the 'identification' stage of the verification process would now involve a substantive judgement and would therefore move beyond the mandate of the Consultative Committee. This Committee would no longer be able to establish a *prima facie* case for a violation of the Convention on the basis of factual evidence alone. From the narrow perspective of verification this shifting of the identification function from a matter of fact to a matter of judgement would seem to represent a loss of precision. But precision in verification is not the only criterion by which such a change must be evaluated, and there may be other points of view from which the increased generality of the prohibition would be seen as a gain.

The above considerations lead to the conclusion that a good case can be made for dropping the threshold provision. If precision in verification had a high priority, then this abandonment of the threshold should be accompanied by an attempt to specify a list of activities prohibited at any level of effect. If technological advances were to make this list inadequate at some later time, new prohibitions could be discussed at future review conferences and added through the established amendment process (article VI). There is, of course, the option of having it both ways, listing some specified activities which are absolutely forbidden and retaining the threshold provision for the rest. This would make the treaty more complex, but the price may be a small one considering the small number of feasible techniques. Finally, if the technical precision of verification is perceived to be of lesser value than the political and symbolic benefits to be gained from a broad, all-inclusive prohibition, then neither a threshold nor a specified list of prohibited techniques would be needed.

The next set of possible extensions of the Enmod Convention involves the prohibition or limitation of research, development, production and possession of environmental modification technologies. Here again there appears to be no general prescription which will work for all cases, but some suggestions can be made. The essence of the problem lies in the essentially *ad hoc*, as opposed to continuous, provisions in the Convention for verifying compliance. Under the present article V there is no monitoring or inspection unless a complaint is filed, and then, since incriminating evidence can presumably be found on the territory of the complaining party, there should be no problem in getting approval for on-site inspection.

If the Enmod Convention were extended to prohibit research, development, production or possession of environmental modification technologies, the evidence for violation would then have to be found on the territory of the accused state, and this is certain to raise all of the traditional obstacles associated with proposals for on-site inspection. It may be possible in some cases to find certain kinds of evidence outside the boundaries of the accused state. These are, after all, environmental modification techniques, the effects of which might well spread beyond national boundaries. Such effects could be looked for on an *ad hoc* basis as long as neighbouring states were willing to allow inspections, but it is possible to imagine plausible scenarios when even this would not be permitted.

One alternative is for the Enmod Convention to be modified to include provisions for continuous or periodic monitoring using technical means under the control of an international scientific group or an intergovernmental agency such as the office of the United Nations Secretary-General. In this version of the Convention the *ad hoc* Consultative Committee of Experts would be replaced by a permanent verification agency. Such an agency would require technical and scientific capability in order to monitor, analyse and identify possible violations. The placing of such capabilities under international control has already been suggested in such currently pending proposals as the one for an International Satellite Monitoring Agency (Bortzmeyer *et al.*, 1983) and an International Seismic Identification Network (Dahlman *et al.*, 1984). Certainly if such mechanisms were politically acceptable, the Enmod Convention would be an excellent place to apply them. But so far these ideas have not proved acceptable to those states which have the most power to prevent them, and it is not clear that the Enmod Convention is the appropriate place to attempt such important innovations.

A second possible verification mechanism for monitoring prohibitions against research, development, production or possession of environmental modification technologies would be based less on technical methods of remote sensing and more on the gathering and exchange of information. Such a scheme could include a declaration by states party to the Enmod Convention of any research activities in these areas and the placing of these activities under full civilian control with full freedom of information. Any tests of environmental modification techniques could be announced in advance and observers invited from other parties. Stockpiles and production rates for relevant materials and devices could be declared and updated on a regular basis. Finally, some on-site inspections, possibly on a challenge basis, could be provided for in the amended Convention.

This form of monitoring corresponds much more closely to what have come to be called confidence-building measures. Such measures are already in the public domain under the 1975 Helsinki agreements for security and co-operation in Europe (Goldblat, 1982, pages 216–217), and a similar collection of measures is under active consideration in the negotiations at the Geneva Conference on Disarmament for a ban on chemical weapons. They seem better suited to the needs of an environmental modification convention than do the expensive, highly technical and continuous remote-sensing devices. However, they do require the creation of a substantial administrative and technical infrastructure, and it must be asked whether the benefits to be gained from extending the Enmod Convention to limitations on research, development, production and possession of environmental modification techniques would be worth the substantial costs of such an infrastructure.

It can be concluded that unless major changes are made in article V of the Enmod Convention it would not be possible to verify with high confidence prohibitions on research, development, production and possession of environmental modification weapons. However, it does not follow from this that these activities should not be prohibited, since any violation would still involve risks of either discovery or suspicion, even without a formal investigation. Verifiability is not the only criterion by which a potential treaty must be judged, and problems of verification cannot be allowed to prevent the world community from condemning activities which are unnecessarily dangerous and destructive. It must also be kept in mind that it is not solely the fear of getting caught which inhibits states from engaging in such activities.

Yet the Enmod Convention seems a poor place to make absolute prohibitions on research, development, production and possession. The problem is that those technologies most likely to be developed are the ones with extensive peaceful applications, such as rain-making and herbicidal techniques. On the other hand, those technologies which would have little or no peaceful use are the ones which are either impossible or highly improbable. There is little to be gained in prohibiting these. Indeed, an attempt to treat environmental modification fantasies as if they were actual possibilities could do real damage to the Convention itself. Therefore any attempt to extend the Convention beyond the prohibition of hostile use of environmental modification techniques would have to make the case either that the political and moral value of these prohibitions would outweigh the substantial technical and administrative costs of verification, or that the broader prohibition would be of sufficient value even without explicit provisions for verification. The experience of the 1972 Bacteriological and Toxin Weapon Convention should lead to caution in choosing the latter alternative.

IV. Conclusion

Arms control has fallen on hard times in the past several years, and in such a situation it is tempting to look for glimmers of hope wherever they might be found. The Enmod Convention may provide such a glimmer, but it is exceedingly faint and largely irrelevant to the truly threatening problems created by the nuclear arms race and by the rapid militarization of so much of world politics. No agreement to prevent certain kinds of destructive activity should be ignored, yet there should also be no illusion that marginal treaties such as the Enmod Convention represent significant progress towards disarmament. They can, in fact, serve as a public relations cover designed to hide the lack of any real progress in this direction.

An analogous phenomenon can be seen in the issue of verification. Although everyone would agree that no treaty is satisfactory if it does not contain adequate provisions to ensure compliance, it is also true that concerns about verifiability can, and in many cases have, become obsessive. Such obsessions can arise from genuine, if somewhat irrational, fears, or they can be cynical tactics whose purpose is to create obstacles to progress in arms control.

Any attempts to revise the Enmod Convention will have to be made in an atmosphere in which irrationality, suspicion and cynicism are stronger than they have been for many years. In such an atmosphere a balanced discussion of compliance issues becomes almost impossible, and even the rather straight-forward extensions considered here will be likely to engender bitter controversy. Nevertheless, there do seem to be ways in which the Enmod Convention could be significantly improved without undue sacrifices in verifiability. Such efforts, if successful, might contribute to a positive modification of the current political environment.

Annex 6.1.   The secret weather war scenario

There are two major questions that can be asked about the likelihood of a long-term covert use by some state of cloud dispersal or rain-making techniques to deprive an unsuspecting enemy of significant quantities of rainfall. The first is whether or not the techniques themselves are feasible; and the second—even if the techniques are assumed to be feasible—is whether such a campaign could be kept secret for a period of at least the several months needed to damage a single harvest or the several years probably needed to create major economic dislocation or famine.

The question of technical feasibility will not be addressed here more than to call attention to the consensus of expert opinion which holds that rain making and cloud dispersal are poorly understood and highly unpredictable techniques (see Westing, chapter 1, section III; Mészáros, chapter 2). For the purposes of this brief analysis it will be assumed that the necessary research has been done and that the basic phenomena are well enough understood that an aggressor wanting to use a technique of this sort would have a reasonable degree of confidence that it would succeed. Any attempt to use the technique without this confidence would in essence amount to combining research, development, deployment and hostile use into the same programme. Given the risk of discovery, the high cost of the programme and the fact that its use would not be an act of desperation, such an effort would defy both common sense and military rationality, even when allowance is made for those areas in which these two criteria do not overlap.

If the technique can be assumed with reasonable confidence to be workable, this confidence would have to have come from an understanding of the basic mechanisms of cloud dispersal and rain formation as well as of the relevant meteorological parameters of the region in which the method was to be deployed. If this knowledge were in the public domain, then the potential victim would be aware of it and would be at least conscious of the possibility that such a technique could be used against it. If the knowledge were not in the public domain, then it would have to have been developed in a secret research and development project which began at some point when the possibility of developing such a technique seemed promising. In either case the international scientific community would already be alert to the danger.

A good analogy for this situation is the research in nuclear physics which took place during the 1930s up until the discovery of nuclear fission. Until this point all nuclear research was in the public domain, and it was precisely at this point that nuclear physicists all over the world simultaneously grasped the potential military significance of nuclear fission. Very soon after this point research into nuclear fission became a secret activity and development of the atomic bomb a real possibility. Different states put different priorities on this effort for a variety of reasons, but from the moment of the discovery of nuclear fission every state had to be alert to the possibility that a potential enemy would develop and use an atomic bomb. Indeed, when Yoshio Nishina, the prominent Japanese physicist, was queried by a military official about Hiroshima shortly after the bombing, he was immediately able to confirm what kind of weapon had been used (Jungk, 1964, page 195).

If it is imagined that such a secret research and development effort were to be undertaken in weather modifiction then it must be assumed that it could be kept secret for the full period of its development. Again, there is the history of the atomic bomb to provide a counter-example. Ironically, it was the very secrecy of the project that alerted the USSR to its existence. The total absence of publications in relevant scientific fields and the disappearance of many important scientists made it clear to Soviet scientists that the USA was working on a nuclear weapon (Holloway, 1979). It may be possible to keep certain details and the rate of progress of such big projects secret for extended periods, but to hide the very fact of the existence of a large-scale climate modification experiment when it involves activities over thousands or tens of thousands of square kilometres, using tens or even hundreds of aircraft, and having effects (e.g., cloud dispersal) visible from satellites stretches credulity beyond reason.

A secret weather modification war could really only be conducted against a neighbouring country, since the effects of modification could only be expected to be controlled over distances comparable to the radius of a weather system—certainly less than 1 000 km, and probably only a few hundred kilometres. If there were a third country in between the attacker and the victim it might also be attacked as an unavoidable consequence of the attack against the intended victim. Such collateral damage is, of course, common in war, but it would add greatly to the risk of serious political consequences if the attack were discovered.

Finally, once the attack began it would involve an extended, systematic, covert programme of aircraft missions within radar range of the attacked state. Radar systems now in regular use by many states have ranges of several hundred kilometres (Pretty, 1984, pages 414–569). The victim would be in a position to observe these flights and correlate them with any anomalous weather patterns over an extended period of time. Although it can be argued that proof of hostile action might be difficult to obtain for a long time, suspicion of hostile action might begin very early; indeed, it might exist even before the attack began. Suspicion would naturally lead to more intensive and systematic monitoring, which in turn would supply more evidence of correlations between certain kinds of aerial activities in the attacking state and certain weather patterns in the attacked state. The more successful the attack in achieving its objectives, the more quickly would convincing evidence of hostile activity accumulate to the point where a protest or countermeasure would be justified.

In order to be able to estimate how difficult the monitoring task might be, some estimate is needed of the scale of the effort which the attacker would have to mount. This would be measured in numbers of aircraft sorties, hours in the air, quantities and types of materials deposited in the clouds, frequency of occurrence of relevant weather systems, and so forth. But since the techniques do not yet exist, such estimates are very difficult to make. A very rough idea can be gained from the following experience (Fedorov, 1975, page 51):

Experiments on cloud dissipation were carried out by Soviet scientists over an area from 3 to 10 thousand square kilometres. For this purpose it was enough to keep in the air 3-4 specially equipped small planes for a few hours.

These planes were, of course, flying directly over the affected area, and there was no implication that the dispersal effects could be made to persist for long distances downwind. If this is taken as an order-of-magnitude estimate of the scale of the effort required to wage a secret weather war, and if the areas to be attacked are measured in the tens of thousands of square kilometres, as they must be if the agriculture of any but the smallest states is to be affected, then it could be estimated that something like 30 "specially equipped" aircraft would have to be in the air for several hours every time a particular set of meteorological conditions existed. This would have to take place within a distance of several hundred kilometres of the regions to be affected, and presumably even closer to the actual boundary of the state being attacked.

Such an exercise would be clearly visible on radar and, since it involved a substantial number of aircraft in the air simultaneously, would be bound to attract the attention of military and civilian air controllers and be recorded by early-warning systems. It is inconceivable that numerous and regular repetitions of such activity would not arouse considerable interest, if not suspicion, from neighbouring states. And once the drought began in earnest it strains credulity to imagine that no one in the attacked state would make the necessary connections.

It might be argued that the US rain-making operation in the Second Indochina War constitutes a refutation of this argument. This programme was reasonably extensive and was carried out over a period of seven years in what seems to have been almost total secrecy. But there is no similarity between this operation and the secret weather war scenario considered here. The rain making in Indochina was carried out as a small component of a vast ground and air war and was designed to stimulate extra rainfall in local areas where the rainfall was already very heavy. However many aircraft sorties were required for the operation, these were dwarfed by the enormous numbers of bombing, transport, combat air support and reconnaissance sorties flown, not to mention the herbicide missions. So the major factor that allowed the Indochina rain-making operation to be kept secret was its relative insignificance in the midst of an already intense war. This is certainly a lesson to be remembered when it comes to future verification of the Enmod Convention during wartime, but it has no relevance to the secret weather war scenario under consideration here.

This analysis leads to the conclusion that the scenario of a secret weather war is highly improbable and not very useful as a motivation for maintaining or extending the Enmod Convention. That scenarios of this sort continue to be resorted to is evidence either of a genuine lack of plausible environmental modification scenarios or of a lack of interest in thinking carefully about how such hostile modifications might be carried out. If the Enmod Convention is to be extended and adequately verified it will be necessary for qualified environmental scientists and arms control experts to devote more effort to identifying plausible violation scenarios and the means by which they might be deterred or detected.

References

ACDA (US Arms Control and Disarmament Agency). 1978. *Environmental Assessment for the Convention on the Prohibition of Military or Any Other Hostile Use of Environmental Modification Techniques*. Washington: US Arms Control & Disarmament Agency. [Reprinted in: Pell, C. (ed.). 1978. *Environmental Modification Treaty* (Hearing, 3 Oct 78). Washington: US Senate Committee on Foreign Relations, 127 pp.: pp. 87–127.]

Andersson, G., Dominguez, M., Dunn, P. and Imobersteg, U. 1984. *Report of the Specialists Appointed by the Secretary-General to Investigate Allegations by the Islamic Republic of Iran Concerning the Use of Chemical Weapons*. New York: UN Security Council Document No. S/16433 (26 Mar 84), 28 pp.

Bortzmeyer, H. G. *et al.* 1983. *Implications of Establishing an International Satellite Monitoring Agency*. New York: UN Department for Disarmament Affairs Disarmament Study Series No. 9, 110 pp.

Canada. 1975. *Suggested Preliminary Approach to Considering the Possibility of Concluding a Convention on the Prohibition of Environmental Modification for Military or Other Hostile Purposes*. Geneva: Conference of the Committee on Disarmament Document No. CCD/463 (5 Aug 75), 24 + 1 pp.

CCD (Conference of the Committee on Disarmament). 1976. *Final Record of the Six Hundred and Ninety-Seventh Meeting*. Geneva: Conference of the Committee on Disarmament Document No. CCD/PV.697 (25 Mar 76), 32 pp.

Dahlman, O. *et al.* 1984. *Third Report to the Conference on Disarmament of the* Ad Hoc *Group of Scientific Experts to Consider International Co-operative Measures to Detect and Identify Seismic Events*. Geneva: Conference on Disarmament Document No. CD/448 (9 Mar 84), 42 pp.

Dore, I. I. 1982. International law and the preservation of the ocean space and outer space as zones of peace: progress and problems. *Cornell International Law Journal*, Ithaca, NY, **15**: 1–61.

Fedorov, E. K. 1975. Disarmament in the field of geophysical weapons. *Scientific World*, London, **19**(3–4): 49–54.

Goldblat, J. 1982. *Agreements for Arms Control: A Critical Survey*. London: Taylor & Francis, 387 pp. [a SIPRI book].

Holloway, D. 1979. *Entering the Nuclear Arms Race: the Soviet Decision to Build the Atomic Bomb, 1939–45*. Washington: Wilson Center International Security Studies Program Working Paper No. 9, 62 pp.

Juda, L. 1978. Negotiating a treaty on environmental modification warfare: the convention on environmental warfare and its impact upon arms control negotiations. *International Organization*, Madison, Wis., **32**: 975–991.

Jungk, R. 1964. *Heller als tausend Sonnen: das Schicksal der Atomforscher* [Brighter than a Thousand Suns: The Fate of the Atomic Scientists]. (In German) Hamburg: Rowohlt, 348 pp.

Kotsch, W. J. 1960. Weather control and national strategy. *United States Naval Institute Proceedings*, Annapolis, Md, **86**(7): 74–81.

MacDonald, G. J. F. 1968. How to wreck the environment. In: Calder, N. (ed.). *Unless Peace Comes: A Scientific Forecast of New Weapons*. London: Allen Lane, 217 pp.: pp. 165–183.

Pretty, R. T. (ed.). 1984. *Jane's Weapon Systems, 1983–84*. 14th ed. London: Jane's Publishing Co., 968 pp.

Sullivan, W. 1983. Scientists ponder forcing asteroids into safe orbits. *New York Times*, 4 Jan: C3, C8.

Sweden, 1975. *Working Paper on Short List of Methods to Influence the Environment for Hostile Purposes*. Geneva: Conference of the Committee on Disarmament Document No. CCD/465 (8 Aug 75), 1 p.

Weiss, E. B. 1975. Weather control: an instrument for war? *Survival*, London, 17(2): 64–68.

Westing, A. H. 1977. Geophysical and environmental weapons. In: SIPRI (eds). *Weapons of Mass Destruction and the Environment*. London: Taylor & Francis, 95 pp: chap. 3 (pp. 49–63).

Wunsch, C. R. 1980. Environmental modification treaty. *A.S.I.L.S. International Law Journal*, Washington, 4: 113–131.

7. Environmental warfare: policy recommendations

The SIPRI/UNIDIR symposium participants[1]

I. Introduction

This final chapter presents a series of policy recommendations dealing with the subject of environmental warfare, in other words, with manipulations of the environment for hostile purposes. All of these recommendations emerge more or less directly from the six foregoing technical, legal and policy appraisals. First there is a short compilation of general recommendations; these are followed by a somewhat smaller number of recommendations that deal specifically with the Environmental Modification (Enmod) Convention of 1977. Many of the proposals put forth could be adopted unilaterally prior to being agreed to among states in treaty form.

II. General recommendations

The following policy recommendations deal with the full range of issues arising from the iniquities of environmental warfare; they refer to both present capabilities and future possibilities. The consequences of a large-scale nuclear war are not dealt with here, but it must be emphasized that such an occurrence would be disastrous to the environment and would place in jeopardy the very survival of our civilization. Indeed, no single action would be more supportive of environmental integrity than a reduction in the risk that nuclear weapons will be used.

1. Release of water

Hundreds of levees, dikes and dams—among them the channel containments of various major rivers as well as more than 70 huge dams in some 20

[1] This chapter was drafted originally by Arthur H. Westing (SIPRI) and then revised at the SIPRI/UNIDIR symposium on 'Environmental warfare' held in Geneva on 24–27 April 1984. It has the endorsement of all of the symposium participants: Richard A. Falk (Princeton University); Jozef Goldblat (SIPRI); Anthony M. Imevbore (University of Ife, Nigeria); Allan S. Krass (Hampshire College, Massachusetts); Ernö Mészáros (Institute for Atmospheric Physics, Budapest); Hallan C. Noltimier (Ohio State University); and Arthur H. Westing (SIPRI).

countries—stand ready to be attacked in time of war. Indeed, some of the most devastating instances of environmental manipulation for military purposes in all human history have involved the breaching of barriers that keep in check the potential energy of streams or other bodies of water. In order to minimize repetitions of such militarily attractive acts against these natural or artefactual components of our environment, it is recommended: (*a*) that human habitations and the products of other capital- or labour-intensive endeavours be kept out of the potential path of at least the water that could be released from the most vulnerable of such barriers; (*b*) that more nations be encouraged to become parties to Protocol I of 1977 Additional to the Geneva Conventions of 1949 which, with certain provisos, prohibits attacks on such structures (for the text of this Protocol, see appendix 3, section I [see especially article 56]; for its parties, see appendix 3, section II); and (*c*) that the parties to this Protocol be encouraged to strengthen the prohibition by making it unconditional (*inter alia*, by unilaterally waiving the provisos contained in article 56.2 and, subsequently, removing them altogether through amendment of the Protocol).

2. Release of radioactivity

Well over 300 major facilities containing huge quantities of radioactive materials—nuclear power stations and such other nuclear facilities as spent-fuel reprocessing plants, nuclear bomb factories and nuclear-waste storage repositories—have been constructed in some 25 countries in recent decades, to become essentially permanent additions to the human environment. These could be attacked, thereby quite possibly releasing their highly dangerous pent-up radioactive energy over a great area and making it uninhabitable for many decades. In order to minimize the possibility of such a manipulation of our environment for hostile purposes it is recommended: (*a*) that any new such facilities be constructed in a manner that takes into account potential environmental consequences; (*b*) that, insofar as possible, all such facilities be kept distinct and at a distance from potential military targets; (*c*) that nations be encouraged to become parties to Protocol I of 1977 Additional to the Geneva Conventions of 1949 which, with certain provisos, prohibits attacks on nuclear electrical generating stations (for the text of this Protocol, see appendix 3, section I [see especially article 56]; for its parties, see appendix 3, section II); and (*d*) that the parties to this treaty be encouraged to strengthen the prohibition by making it unconditional (*inter alia*, by bringing under protection all major facilities containing radioactive materials and by unilaterally waiving the provisos contained in article 56.2 and, subsequently, removing them altogether through amendment of the Protocol).

3. Release of micro-organisms

Virulent and tenacious micro-organisms, such as the causative agent of anthrax, could be introduced into the environment of a country as an act of war. Such a hostile military manipulation of the biotic component of our environment could

84

cause large regions to become unusable for livestock, and even uninhabitable by humans, for decades. In an attempt to preclude such acts of war it is recommended: (*a*) that the already widely adopted Geneva Protocol of 1925 which prohibits the use in war of biological agents, and the almost equally widely adopted Bacteriological and Toxin Weapon Convention of 1972 which prohibits even their possession, be universally adhered to; (*b*) that the parties to these two treaties develop and adopt appropriate procedures for verification of compliance and for dealing with allegations of breaches; (*c*) that nations be encouraged to become parties to the Enmod Convention of 1977 which, with certain provisos, prohibits the deliberate manipulation for hostile purposes of the composition and dynamics of the biota (for the text of this Convention, see appendix 2, section I; for its parties, see appendix 2, section II); and (*d*) that the parties to this treaty strengthen it in ways suggested in section III below.

4. Protection of special regions

A very modest number of geographical regions are protected by multilateral treaty from all of the insults of war—and thus also from any hostile military manipulations of the environment. The most prominent example is the Antarctic continent and perijacent waters, through the Antarctic Treaty of 1959. It is recommended: (*a*) that this treaty be more widely adhered to; (*b*) that it be amended so as to remove the preferential treatment given to certain nations; (*c*) that Antarctica be formally recognized as a common heritage of humankind; and (*d*) that additional geographical areas be created as sanctuaries from environmental or other warfare. Special consideration for the establishment of such demilitarized regions shold be given: (*a*) to regions of geological instability, for example, containing active volcanoes, polar ice sheets, thixotropic soils (soils that became fluid during the time they are subjected to vibration) or active fault zones (fractures in the Earth's crust); and (*b*) to ecologically important regions, that is to say, those regions that (i) contribute substantially to the global balance of nature, (ii) contain intrinsically fragile ecosystems, (iii) support unique habitats, or (iv) provide the habitat for species in danger of extinction.

5. Environmental modifications

It is to some extent already possible to manipulate certain major forces of nature, a class of capabilities that is certain to be developed more fully in the years to come. These capabilities, present and future, might include techniques for changing—through the deliberate manipulation of natural processes—the dynamics, composition or structure of space or of the Earth, including its atmosphere, lithosphere, hydrosphere or biosphere (biota). In order to help prevent destructive actions of this sort it is recommended: (*a*) that the Enmod Convention of 1977—which proscribes such activities so long as they (i) have been carried out deliberately for hostile purposes, and (ii) have what are referred to as widespread, long-lasting or severe effects—be more widely adhered to (for the text of this Convention, see appendix 2, section I; for its parties, see appendix 2, section II); and (*b*) that the parties to this treaty strengthen it in ways suggested in section III below.

6. Research, development and monitoring

A number of grandiose environmental modifications could serve beneficial purposes once the underlying processes were adequately understood and the means of control sufficiently developed. These might include modifications of rainfall, of wind storms or of tectonic activity. In order to help allay the fear that such capabilities were being pursued for hostile military purposes, it is recommended: (*a*) that all relevant research, development and monitoring be carried out openly and within the civil sector; (*b*) that environmental impact statements or technology assessments be carried out under international auspices prior to testing; and (*c*) that all relevant tests be announced and made accessible to international observation.

III. Recommendations relating to the Environmental Modification Convention

In paragraphs 3 and 5 of section II above it was recommended that the Enmod Convention be more widely adhered to and that it be improved in certain ways. The following policy recommendations are meant to strengthen this Convention which, as it stands, prohibits the manipulation of natural processes of the environment for hostile purposes only in a circumscribed and limited fashion.

1. The Understandings

The Enmod Convention is vague in several respects. In order to help remedy this shortcoming, it is recommended that most of the so-called Understandings to the Convention be made an integral part of it (for the text of the Understandings, see appendix 2, section III).

2. The threshold

The Enmod Convention prohibits environmental modifications only if their effect were to achieve widespread, long-lasting or severe proportions. This threshold is not defined in the Convention (and only inadequately in the unofficial Understandings) and is at best subject to considerable uncertainty and ambiguity. Moreover, in permitting some level of manipulation of the environment for hostile purposes, the Convention, in fact, condones military preparations for, and the actual perpetration of, these activities. In order to remedy this salient flaw in the Convention, it is strongly recommended that the threshold simply be struck from it (an amendment of article I that would, of course, make the Understanding relating to this article unnecessary). Deletion of the threshold would be the single most important means of improving the Enmod Convention, transforming it from an ambiguous and cumbersome instrument of modest value to a meaningful component of both the arms control and environmental protection regimes.

3. Hostile intent

The Enmod Convention prohibits environmental manipulations only when they are carried out with the deliberate intent to change natural processes for hostile purposes. Such deliberate hostile intent could be difficult to establish in the absence of an admission by the perpetrator. It is therefore recommended that the Convention be amended to extend the existing prohibition to include any hostile environmental manipulation that could be reasonably expected to result in a prohibited effect even if the environmental modification was not meant as the primary form of attack (as already suggested in part in the Understanding relating to article II).

4. Development

The Enmod Convention contains restrictions on the use of environmental modification techniques for hostile purposes, but not on their development. Thus, in order to elevate the Convention from a mere law of armed conflict to a real instrument of arms control, it is recommended: (a) that the Convention be amended to prohibit all militarily oriented development of environmental modification techniques (and that such amendment be supported by appropriate acts of national legislation); and (b) that the monitoring of compliance with such a restriction be carried out under international auspices, in conjunction with the monitoring of the relevant peaceful pursuits referred to in paragraph 6 of section II above.

5. Universality

The Enmod Convention limits environmental modifications for hostile purposes only among the parties. By tolerating the carrying out of such environmental modifications against other nations it again condones military preparations for, and the actual perpetration of, these activities. Moreover, this permissive aspect of the Convention exists even though the primary impact of the proscribed actions would be expected to be on the civilian population of the attacked nation and its environment, and might well also extend to third parties or the common domain. It is thus recommended that the Convention be amended so that the acts themselves are prohibited irrespective of the party status of a potential victim.

IV. Conclusion

Manipulations of the environment for hostile military purposes have had spectacularly devastating results in the past, whether measured in terms of civilian fatalities, material damage or ecological impact. The future will certainly bring us even greater abilities to effectively manipulate the potentially dangerous forces that are pent-up in the environment. Thus our modifications of the global environment must be dedicated to the benefit of humankind and nature. They must be carried out in good faith, facilitated by international understanding and co-operation and in the spirit of good neighbourliness—as has been recommended by the United Nations Environment Programme (UNEP, 1980).

The global environment is being subjected to ever more serious strains by a growing world population that seeks at least the basic necessities of life as well as some of its amenities. In order to help ensure that the increasingly limited resources of our environment are not further reduced by hostile military activities, it is urged that environmental issues in general and those raised by environmental warfare in particular be widely publicized, through schools and by other means, in order to help develop and strengthen cultural norms in opposition to military activities that cause direct or indirect environmental harm.

In closing it is thus recommended that all nations recognize their responsibility towards nature as embodied in such widely endorsed documents as the Declaration of the United Nations Conference on the Human Environment of 1972 (UNGA, 1973) and the World Charter for Nature of 1982 (UNGA, 1982) including, *inter alia*, their responsibility: (*a*) to ensure that activities within their jurisdiction or control do not cause damage to the environment in other states or in areas beyond the limits of national jurisdiction; and (*b*) to avoid military activities damaging to nature anywhere.

References

UNEP (United Nations Environment Programme). 1980. *Earthwatch: Assessment of Outer Limits: Provisions for Co-operation between States in Weather Modification*. Nairobi: UN Environment Programme Resolution No. 8/7.A (29 Apr 80), 2 pp.

UNGA (United Nations General Assembly). 1973. *Report of the United Nations Conference on the Human Environment, Stockholm 5–16 June 1972*. New York: UN General Assembly Document No. A/CONF.48/14/Rev. 1, 77 pp. Resolution No. 2994(XXVII) (15 Dec 72), 2 pp.]

UNGA (United Nations General Assembly). 1982. *World Charter for Nature*. New York: UN General Assembly Resolution No. 37/7 (28 Nov 82), 5 pp.

Appendix 1.   Environmental warfare (technical, legal and policy aspects): select bibliography

Arthur H. Westing
Stockholm International Peace Research Institute

Albrecht, U. 1983. Wetter-Rüsten [Preparing for weather warfare]. (In German) *Natur*, Munich, 8 Aug: 50–59, 102–103.

Arms Control and Disarmament Agency, US. 1976. *Environmental Warfare: Questions and Answers*. Washington: US Arms Control & Disarmament Agency Publication No. 83, 10 pp.

Arms Control and Disarmament Agency, US. 1978. *Environmental Assessment for the Convention on the Prohibition of Military or Any Other Hostile Use of Environmental Modification Techniques*. Washington: US Arms Control & Disarmament Agency. [Reprinted in: Pell, C. (ed.). 1978. *Environmental Modification Treaty* (Hearing, 3 Oct 78). Washington: US Senate Committee on Foreign Relations, 127 pp.: pp. 87–127.]

Arms Control and Disarmament Agency, US. 1982. Convention on the Prohibition of Military or any other Hostile Use of Environmental Modification Techniques. In: *Arms Control and Disarmament Agreements*. Washington: US Arms Control & Disarmament Agency, 290 pp.: pp. 190–200.

Barnaby, F. 1976. Environmental warfare. *Bulletin of the Atomic Scientists*, Chicago, **32**(5): 36–43.

Begishev, V. 1972. Another genocide weapon. *New Times*, Moscow, **1972**(32): 26–27.

Berberović, L. 1979. [On the concepts, forms and means of ecocide.] (In Serbo-Croat) *Vojno Delo*, Belgrade, **31**(4): 79–91.

Breuer, G. 1980. *Weather Modification: Prospects and Problems*. (Translated from the German by H. Mörth) Cambridge, UK: Cambridge University Press, 178 pp. (Hostile military weather modification, pp. 70–74, 144–151) Originally: *Wetter nach Wunsch?* [Weather to order?]. Stuttgart: Deutsche Verlags-Anstalt, 180 pp., 1976.

Canada. 1975.; *Suggested Preliminary Approach to Considering the Possibility of Concluding a Convention on the Prohibition of Environmental Modification for Military or Other Hostile Purposes*. Geneva: Conference of the Committee on Disarmament Document No. CCD/463 (5 Aug 75), 24 + 1 pp.

CCD (Committee of the Conference on Disarmament). 1976. *Report of the Working Group on the Prohibition of Military or any Other Hostile Use of Environmental Modification Techniques to the Plenary of the CCD*. Geneva: Committee of the Conference on Disarmament Document No. CCD/520 (3 Sep 76), [131] pp.: Annex A (13 pp). [Reprinted in: New York: UN General Assembly Document No. A/31/27, Suppl. 27, Vol. 1, 107 pp.: pp. 86–96; 1976. See also: UN General Assembly Resolution No. 31/72 (10 Dec 76), 5 pp.]

Clark, W. H. 1961. Chemical and thermonuclear explosives. *Bulletin of the Atomic Scientists*, Chicago, **17**: 356–360.

Davis, R. J. 1972. Weather warfare: law and policy. *Arizona Law Review*, Tucson, **14**: 659–688.

Falk, R. A. 1973. Environmental warfare and ecocide. *Bulletin of Peace Proposals*, Oslo, **4**: 1–17. [Also in: *Revue Belge de Droit International*, Brussels, **9**(1): 1–27.]

Fedorov, E. K. 1975. Disarmament in the field of geophysical weapons. *Scientific World*, London, **19**(3–4): 49–54.

Fischer, G. 1977. Convention sur l'interdiction d'utiliser des techniques de modification de l'environement à des fins hostiles [Convention on the prohibition of the utilization of techniques to modify the environment for hostile purposes]. (In French) *Annuaire Français de Droit International*, Paris, **23**: 820-836.

Friedman, R. 1976-77. Earthquake warfare: preliminary report on Pentagon's unthinkable plans. *CounterSpy Magazine*, Washington, 3(2): 26.

Ghosh, S. K. 1976. Environmental warfare. *Institute for Defence Studies & Analyses News Review on Science and Technology*, New Delhi, May: 219-222.

Goeckel, K. 1980. Science fiction in der Kriegführung: Verbot der Umweltveränderung zu feindseligen Zwecken [Science fiction in warfare: prohibition of environmental modification for hostile purposes]. (In German) *Zivilverteidigung*, Bad Honnef, FR Germany, **1980**(3): 33-39.

Golab, Z. 1981. [Chemical, 'meteorological', and 'geophysical' weapons as well as incendiary means in local wars.] (In Polish) *Mysl Wojskowa*, Warsaw, **37**(1): 93-104.

Goldblat, J. 1975. Prohibition of environmental means of warfare. In: SIPRI (eds). *World Armaments and Disarmament, SIPRI Yearbook 1975*, Stockholm: Almqvist & Wiksell, pp. 432-436.

Goldblat, J. 1975. Prohibition of environmental warfare. *Ambio*, Stockholm, **4**: 186-190.

Goldblat, J. 1976. Prohibition of environmental means of warfare. In: SIPRI (eds). *World Armaments and Disarmament, SIPRI Yearbook 1976*, Stockholm: Almqvist & Wiksell, pp. 314-323.

Goldblat, J. 1977. Environmental warfare convention: how meaningful is it? *Ambio*, Stockholm, **6**: 216-221.

Goldblat, J. 1978. Environmental weapons. In: SIPRI (eds). *World Armaments and Disarmament, SIPRI Yearbook 1978*, London: Taylor & Francis pp. 377-382, 392-397.

Goldblat, J. 1982. ENMOD Convention. In: Goldblat, J. (ed.). *Agreements for Arms Control: A Critical Survey*. London: Taylor & Francis, 387 pp.: pp. 51-53, 228-231, 303-335. [a SIPRI book].

Granville, P. 1975. Perspectives de la guerre météorologique et géophysique: un exemple concret: les opérations de pluies provoquées en Indochine [Perspectives on meteorological and geophysical warfare: a concrete example: the rainmaking operations in Indochina]. (In French) *Défense Nationale*, Paris, **31**(1): 125-140.

Hecht, R. 1976. Zur Frage eines Umweltkrieges [On the question of an environmental war]. (In German) *Österreichische Militärische Zeitschrift*, Vienna, **14**: 114-115.

Höchner, K. M. 1977. *Schutz der Umwelt im Kriegsrecht [Protection of the environment in the law of war]*. (In German) Zurich: Schulthess Polygraphischer Verlag, 154 pp.

Horton, A. M. 1975. Weather modification: a Pandora's box? *Air Force Magazine*, Washington, **58**(2): 36-40.

Hoyle, T. 1983. *Last Gasp*. New York: Crown Publishers, 430 pp.

Iojrysh, A. I. 1977. [Prohibition of the military use of the environment.] (In Russian) *Sovetskoe Gosudarstvo i Pravo*, Moscow, **1977**(12): 66-70.

Israelyan, V. 1974. New Soviet initiative on disarmament. *International Affairs*, Moscow, **1974**(11): 19-25.

Jasani, B. M. 1975. Environmental modification: new weapons of war? *Ambio*, Stockholm, **4**: 191-198. [Similar in: SIPRI (eds). *World Armaments and Disarmament, SIPRI Yearbook 1976*, Stockholm: Almqvist & Wiksell pp. 72-86.]

Juda, L. 1978. Negotiating a treaty on environmental modification warfare: the convention on environmental warfare and its impact upon arms control negotiations. *International Organization*, Madison, Wis., **32**: 975-991.

Kotsch, W. J. 1960. Weather control and national strategy. *United States Naval Institute Proceedings*, Annapolis, Md., **86**(7): 74-81.

Kozicki, S. 1975. [Some aspects of the possibility to deliberately influence the natural environment for military purposes.] (In Polish) *Mysl Wojskowa*, Warsaw, **31**(2): 9-16.

MacDonald, G. J. F. 1968. How to wreck the environment. In: Calder, N. (ed.). *Unless Peace Comes: A Scientific Forecast of New Weapons*. London: Allen Lane, 217 pp.: pp. 165-183.

MacDonald, G. J. 1975-76. Weather modification as a weapon. *Technology Review*, Cambridge, Mass., **78**(1-2): 56-63.

Maksimov, N. 1978. [Work done abroad on the development of new types of weapons based on new principles.] (In Russian) *Zarubezhnoe Voennoe Obozrenie*, Moscow, **1978**(4): 14-19.

Mattes, M. A. and Bothe, M. 1975. Draft convention on environmental warfare offered at disarmament conference. *Environmental Policy and Law*, Amsterdam, **1**(3): 136-137.

Muntz, J. 1978. Environmental modification. *Harvard International Law Journal*, Cambridge, Mass., **19**: 384–389.

Pell, C. (ed.). 1974. *Weather Modification* [Hearings, 25 Jan and 20 Mar 74]. Washington: US Senate Committee on Foreign Relations, 123 pp.

Ponte, L. 1976. Weather, climate, and war. In: *Cooling*. Englewood Cliffs, N.J.: Prentice-Hall, 306 pp.: chap. 11 (pp. 159–174).

Poppei, G. 1979. Secondary environmental weapons. *Scientific World*, London, **23**(4): 17–18.

Ritchie, D. J. 1959. Reds may use lightning as weapon. *Missiles and Rockets*, Washington, **5**(35): 13–14.

Rognedin, I. 1974. [Geophysical warfare: reality and possibilities.] (In Russian) *Voennaya Mysl*, Moscow, **1974**(10): 92–96.

Schneider, M. M. 1976. Gegen den militärischen Mißbrauch der Umwelt [Against the military misuse of the environment]. (In German) *Deutsche Außenpolitik*, East Berlin, **21**: 578–601.

Schneider, M. M. 1976. Zum Begriff der Umweltkriegführung aus der Sicht der internationalen Anstrengungen um ihr Verbot [Towards an understanding of environmental warfare from the viewpoint of efforts at its prohibition]. (In German) *Sitzungsberichte der Akademie der Wissenschaften der DDR*, East Berlin, **1976**(13N): 26–32.

Sion, I. G. 1980. Ecological imperatives and the need for a political–juridical strategy in the field of disarmament. *Revue Roumaine d'Etudes Internationales*, Bucharest, **14**(4): 356–361.

Studer, T. A. 1968–69. Weather modification in support of military operations. *Air University Review*, Maxwell Air Force Base, Ala., **20**(6): 44–50.

Sullivan, W. 1975. Ozone depletion seen as a war tool. *New York Times*, 28 Feb: 20.

Sullivan, W. 1983. Scientists ponder forcing asteroids into safe orbits. *New York Times*, 4 Jan: C3, C8.

UN. 1976. Convention on the prohibition of military or any other hostile use of environmental modification techniques. *UN Disarmament Yearbook*, New York, **1**: 179–190, 287–295.

Vance, C. R. 1977. United States signs convention banning environmental warfare. *Department of State Bulletin*, Washington, **76**: 633–634.

Vucinić, M. 1978. [Possibilities of the use of environmental modifications for war purposes.] (In Serbo-Croat) *Vojno Delo*, Belgrade, **30**(5): 145–159.

Weiss, E. B. 1974. Weather as a weapon. In: Russell, R. B. (ed.) *Air, Water, Earth, Fire: The Impact of the Military on World Environmental Order*. San Francisco: Sierra Club International Series No. 2, 71 pp.: chap. 5 (pp. 51–62).

Weiss, E. B. 1975. Weather control: an instrument for war? *Survival*, London, **17**(2): 64–68.

Westing, A. H. 1974. Proscription of ecocide: arms control and the environment. *Bulletin of the Atomic Scientists*, Chicago, **30**(1): 24–27.

Westing, A. H. 1976. In: SIPRI (eds). *Ecological Consequences of the Second Indochina War*. Stockholm: Almqvist & Wiksell, 119 pp. + 8 pl.

Westing, A. H. 1977. Geophysical and environmental weapons. In: SIPRI (eds). *Weapons of Mass Destruction and the Environment*. London: Taylor & Francis, 95 pp.: chap. 3 (pp. 49–63).

Wunsch, C. R. 1980. Environmental modification treaty. *A.S.I.L.S. International Law Journal*, Washington, **4**: 113–131.

Appendix 2. The Environmental Modification Convention of 1977

I. Text

The Convention on the Prohibition of Military or any other Hostile Use of Environmental Modification Techniques (or Enmod Convention) was signed at Geneva on 18 May 1977 and (the United Nations Secretary-General, the depositary, having received the requisite 20 ratifications) entered into force on 5 October 1978. The parties to the Convention are given in section II below. A series of Understandings provided by the framers of the Convention are given in section III below. The text of the Convention follows (ACDA, 1979, pages 322–326):

The States Parties to this Convention,

Guided by the interest of consolidating peace, and wishing to contribute to the cause of halting the arms race, and of bringing about general and complete disarmament under strict and effective international control, and of saving mankind from the danger of using new means of warfare,

Determined to continue negotiations with a view to achieving effective progress towards further measures in the field of disarmament,

Recognizing that scientific and technical advances may open new possibilities with respect to modification of the environment,

Recalling the Declaration of the United Nations Conference on the Human Environment, adopted at Stockholm on 16 June 1972,

Realizing that the use of environmental modification techniques for peaceful purposes could improve the interrelationship of man and nature and contribute to the preservation and improvement of the environment for the benefit of present and future generations,

Recognizing, however, that military or any other hostile use of such techniques could have effects extremely harmful to human welfare,

Desiring to prohibit effectively military or any other hostile use of environmental modification techniques in order to eliminate the dangers to mankind from such use, and affirming their willingness to work towards the achievement of this objective,

Desiring also to contribute to the strengthening of trust among nations and to the further improvement of the international situation in accordance with the purposes and principles of the Charter of the United Nations,

Have agreed as follows:

Article I

1. Each State Party to this Convention undertakes not to engage in military or any other hostile use of environmental modification techniques having widespread, long-lasting or severe effects as the means of destruction, damage or injury to any other State Party.

2. Each State Party to this Convention undertakes not to assist, encourage or induce any State, group of States or international organization to engage in activities contrary to the provisions of paragraph 1 of this article.

Article II

As used in article I, the term "environmental modification techniques" refers to any technique for changing—through the deliberate manipulation of natural processes—the dynamics, composition or structure of the earth, including its biota, lithosphere, hydrosphere and atmosphere, or of outer space.

Article III

1. The provisions of this Convention shall not hinder the use of environmental modification techniques for peaceful purposes and shall be without prejudice to the generally recognized principles and applicable rules of international law concerning such use.

2. The States Parties to this Convention undertake to facilitate, and have the right to participate in, the fullest possible exchange of scientific and technological information on the use of environmental modification techniques for peaceful purposes. States Parties in a position to do so shall contribute, alone or together with other States or international organizations, to international economic and scientific co-operation in the preservation, improvement and peaceful utilization of the environment, with due consideration for the needs of the developing areas of the world.

Article IV

Each State Party to this Convention undertakes to take any measures it considers necessary in accordance with its constitutional processes to prohibit and prevent any activity in violation of the provisions of the Convention anywhere under its jurisdiction or control.

Article V

1. The States Parties to this Convention undertake to consult one another and to co-operate in solving any problems which may arise in relation to the objectives of, or in the application of the provisions of, the Convention. Consultation and co-operation pursuant to this article may also be undertaken through appropriate international procedures within the framework of the United Nations and in accordance with its Charter. These international procedures may include the services of appropriate international organizations, as well as of a Consultative Committee of Experts as provided for in paragraph 2 of this article.

2. For the purposes set forth in paragraph 1 of this article, the Depositary shall, within one month of the receipt of a request from any State Party to this Convention, convene a Consultative Committee of Experts. Any State Party may appoint an expert to the Committee whose functions and rules of procedure are set out in the annex, which constitutes an integral part of this Convention. The Committee shall transmit to the

Depositary a summary of its findings of fact, incorporating all views and information presented to the Committee during its proceedings. The Depositary shall distribute the summary to all States Parties.

3. Any State Party to this Convention which has reason to believe that any other State Party is acting in breach of obligations deriving from the provisions of the Convention may lodge a complaint with the Security Council of the United Nations. Such a complaint should include all relevant information as well as all possible evidence supporting its validity.

4. Each State Party to this Convention undertakes to co-operate in carrying out any investigation which the Security Council may initiate, in accordance with the provisions of the Charter of the United Nations, on the basis of the complaint received by the Council. The Security Council shall inform the States Parties of the results of the investigation.

5. Each State Party to this Convention undertakes to provide or support assistance, in accordance with the provisions of the Charter of the United Nations, to any State Party which so requests, if the Security Council decides that such Party has been harmed or is likely to be harmed as a result of violation of the Convention.

Article VI

1. Any State Party to this Convention may propose amendments to the Convention. The text of any proposed amendment shall be submitted to the Depositary, who shall promptly circulate it to all States Parties.

2. An amendment shall enter into force for all States Parties to this Convention which have accepted it, upon the deposit with the Depositary of instruments of acceptance by a majority of States Parties. Thereafter it shall enter in force for any remaining State Party on the date of deposit of its instrument of acceptance.

Article VII

This Convention shall be of unlimited duration.

Article VIII

1. Five years after the entry into force of this Convention, a conference of the States Parties to the Convention shall be covened by the Depositary at Geneva, Switzerland. The conference shall review the operation of the Convention with a view to ensuring that its purposes and provisions are being realized, and shall in particular examine the effectiveness of the provisions of paragraph 1 of article I in eliminating the dangers of military or any other hostile use of environmental modification techniques.

2. At intervals of not less than five years thereafter, a majority of the States Parties to this Convention may obtain, by submitting a proposal to this effect to the Depositary, the convening of a conference with the same objectives.

3. If no conference has been convened pursuant to paragraph 2 of this article within ten years following the conclusion of a previous conference, the Depositary shall solicit the views of all States Parties to this Convention, concerning the convening of such a conference. If one third or ten of the States Parties, whichever number is less, respond affirmatively, the Depositary shall take immediate steps to convene the conference.

Article IX

1. This Convention shall be open to all States for signature. Any State which does not sign the Convention before its entry into force in accordance with paragraph 3 of this

article may accede to it at any time.

2. This Convention shall be subject to ratification by signatory States. Instruments of ratification or accession shall be deposited with the Secretary-General of the United Nations.

3. This Convention shall enter into force upon the deposit of instruments of ratification by twenty Governments in accordance with paragraph 2 of this article.

4. For those States whose instruments of ratification or accession are deposited after the entry into force of this Convention, it shall enter into force on the date of the deposit of their instruments of ratification or accession.

5. The Depositary shall promptly inform all signatory and acceding States of the date of each signature, the date of deposit of each instrument of ratification or accession and the date of the entry into force of this Convention and of any amendments thereto, as well as of the receipt of other notices.

6. This Convention shall be registered by the Depositary in accordance with Article 102 of the Charter of the United Nations.

Article X

The Convention, of which the English, Arabic, Chinese, French, Russian and Spanish texts are equally authentic, shall be deposited with the Secretary-General of the United Nations, who shall send duly certified copies thereof to the Governments of the signatory and acceding States.

In witness whereof, the undersigned, being duly authorized thereto by their respective Governments, have signed this Convention, opened for signature at Geneva on the eighteenth day of May, one thousand nine hundred and seventy-seven.

ANNEX

Consultative Committee of Experts

1. The Consultative Committee of Experts shall undertake to make appropriate findings of fact and provide expert views relevant to any problem raised pursuant to paragraph 1 of article V of this Convention by the State Party requesting the convening of the Committee.

2. The work of the Consultative Committee of Experts shall be organized in such a way as to permit it to perform the functions set forth in paragraph 1 of this annex. The Committee shall decide procedural questions relative to the organization of its work, where possible by consensus, but otherwise by a majority of those present and voting. There shall be no voting on matters of substance.

3. The Depositary or his representative shall serve as the Chairman of the Committee.

4. Each expert may be assisted at meetings by one or more advisers.

5. Each expert shall have the right, through the Chairman, to request from States, and from international organizations, such information and assistance as the expert considers desirable for the accomplishment of the Committee's work.

II. Parties

As of April 1984, the Enmod Convention has accumulated a total of 43 parties (this sum including Byelorussia and the Ukraine, both constituent republics of the

USSR). Of the five permanent members of the United Nations Security Council, so far the UK, the USA and the USSR have become parties, whereas China and France have not. A list of all 43 of the parties to the Convention as of April 1984, together with their year of joining, follows (Goldblat and Ferm, 1984, pages 653ff):

Bangladesh (1979), Belgium (1982), Bulgaria (1978), Byelorussia (1978), Canada (1981), Cape Verde (1979), Cuba (1978), Cyprus (1978), Czechoslovakia (1978), Denmark (1978), Egypt (1982), Finland (1978), German DR (1978), Germany, FR (1983), Ghana (1978), Greece (1983), Hungary (1978), India (1978), Ireland (1982), Italy (1981), Japan (1982), Kuwait (1980), Laos (1978), Malawi (1978), Mongolia (1978), Netherlands (1983), Norway (1979), Papua New Guinea (1980), Poland (1978), Romania (1983), Sao Tomé & Principe (1979), Solomon Islands (1981), Spain (1978), Sri Lanka (1978), Sweden (1984), Tunisia (1978), Ukraine (1978), United Kingdom (1978), USA (1980), USSR (1978), Viet Nam (1980), Yemen AR (1977), and Yemen, PDR (1979).

III. Understandings

The Conference of the Committee on Disarmament (CCD), the drafter of the Enmod Convention, worked out a series of four so-called Understandings in explanation and amplification of portions of the Convention. These Understandings, which are *not* a part of the Convention, follow (CCD, 1976, pages 6–7):

Understanding relating to Article I

It is the understanding of the Committee that, for the purposes of this Convention, the terms "widespread", "long-lasting" and "severe" shall be interpreted as follows:
  (a) "widespread": encompassing an area on the scale of several hundred square kilometres;
  (b) "long-lasting": lasting for a period of months, or approximately a season;
  (c) "severe": involving serious or significant disruption of harm to human life, natural and economic resources or other assets.
It is further understood that the interpretation set forth above is intended exclusively for this Convention and is not intended to prejudice the interpretation of the same or similar terms if used in connexion with any other international agreement.

Understanding relating to Article II

It is the understanding of the Committee that the following examples are illustrative of phenomena that could be caused by the use of environmental modification techniques as defined in Article II of the Convention: earthquakes; tsunamis; an upset in the ecological balance of a region; changes in weather patterns (clouds, precipitation, cyclones of various types and tornadic storms); changes in climate patterns; changes in ocean currents; changes in the state of the ozone layer; and changes in the state of the ionosphere.
It is further understood that all the phenomena listed above, when produced by military or any other hostile use of environmental modification techniques, would result, or could reasonably be expected to result, in widespread, long-lasting or severe

destruction, damage or injury. Thus, military or any other hostile use of environmental modification techniques as defined in Article II, so as to cause those phenomena as a means of destruction, damage or injury to another State Party, would be prohibited.

It is recognized, moreover, that the list of examples set out above is not exhaustive. Other phenomena which could result from the use of environmental modification techniques as defined in Article II could also be appropriately included. The absence of such phenomena from the list does not in any way imply that the undertaking contained in Article I would not be applicable to those phenomena, provided the criteria set out in that Article were met.

Understanding relating to Article III

It is the understanding of the Committee that this Convention does not deal with the question whether or not a given use of environmental modification techniques for peaceful purposes is in accordance with generally recognized principles and applicable rules of international law.

Understanding relating to Article VIII

It is the understanding of the Committee that a proposal to amend the Convention may also be considered at any Conference of Parties held pursuant to Article VIII. It is further understood that any proposed amendment that is intended for such consideration should, if possible, be submitted to the Depositary no less than 90 days before the commencement of the Conference.

References

ACDA (US Arms Control and Disarmament Agency). 1979. *Documents on Disarmament 1977.* Washington: US Arms Control and Disarmament Agency Publication No. 101, 922 pp.

CCD (Committee of the Conference on Disarmament). 1976. *Report of the Working Group on the Prohibition of Military or Any Other Hostile Use of Environmental Modification Techniques to the Plenary of the CCD.* Geneva: Committee of the Conference on Disarmament Document No. CCD/520 (3 Sep 76), [131] pp.: Annex A (13 pp.). [Reprinted in: New York: UN General Assembly Document No. A/31/27, Suppl. 27, Vol. 1, 107 pp: pp. 86–96; 1976. See also: UN General Assembly Resolution No. 31/72 (10 Dec 76), 5 pp.]

Goldblat, J. and Ferm, R. 1984. Arms control agreements. In: SIPRI (eds). *World Armaments and Disarmament, SIPRI Yearbook 1984.* London: Taylor & Francis, 700 pp.: 637–676.

Appendix 3. Geneva Protocol I of 1977

I. Text

Protocol I Additional to the Geneva Conventions of 1949, and Relating to the Protection of Victims of International Armed Conflicts was signed at Bern on 12 December 1977 and (the Swiss Federal Council, the depositary, having received the requisite two ratifications) entered into force on 7 December 1978.[1] The parties to the Protocol are given in section II below. Excerpts from the text of the Protocol follow (Roberts and Guelff, 1982, pages 387–446, 459–463):

The High Contracting Parties,
Proclaiming their earnest wish to see peace prevail among peoples,
Recalling that every State has the duty, in conformity with the Charter of the United Nations, to refrain in its international relations from the threat or use of force against the sovereignty, territorial integrity or political independence of any State, or in any other manner inconsistent with the purposes of the United Nations,
Believing it necessary nevertheless to reaffirm and develop the provisions protecting the victims of armed conflicts and to supplement measures intended to reinforce their application,
Expressing their conviction that nothing in this Protocol or in the Geneva Conventions of 12 August 1949 can be construed as legitimizing or authorizing any act of aggression or any other use of force inconsistent with the Charter of the United Nations,
Reaffirming further that the provisions of the Geneva Conventions of 12 August 1949 and of this Protocol must be fully applied in all circumstances to all persons who are protected by those instruments, without any adverse distinction based on the nature or origin of the armed conflict or on the causes espoused by or attributed to the Parties to the conflict,
Have agreed on the following:

. . .

Article 35—Basic rules [with reference to methods and means of warfare]

1. In any armed conflict, the right of the Parties to the conflict to choose methods or means of warfare is not unlimited.

---

[1] There exists a more or less comparable 'Protocol II Additional to the Geneva Conventions of 1949, and Relating to the Protection of Victims of Non-international Armed Conflicts' (Roberts and Guelff, 1982, pages 447–463) which has many of the same, although fewer, parties than Protocol I (ICRC, 1984).

99

2. It is prohibited to employ weapons, projectiles and material and methods of warfare of a nature to cause superfluous injury or unnecessary suffering.

3. It is prohibited to employ methods or means of warfare which are intended, or may be expected, to cause widespread, long-term and severe damage to the natural environment. [See also article 55.1.]

Article 36—New weapons

In the study, development, acquisition or adoption of a new weapon, means or method of warfare, a High Contracting Party is under an obligation to determine whether its employment would, in some or all circumstances, be prohibited by this Protocol or by any other rule of international law applicable to the High Contracting Party.

• • •

Article 48—Basic rule [with reference to the civilian population]

In order to ensure respect for and protection of the civilian population and civilian objects, the Parties to the conflict shall at all times distinguish between the civilian population and combatants and between civilian objects and military objectives and accordingly shall direct their operations only against military objectives.

Article 49—Definition of attacks and scope of application

1. 'Attacks' means acts of violence against the adversary, whether in offence or in defence.

2. The provisions of this Protocol with respect to attacks apply to all attacks in whatever territory conducted, including the national territory belonging to a Party to the conflict but under the control of an adverse Party.

3. The provisions of this Section [on general protection of the civilian population against effects of hostilities; articles 48–67] apply to any land, air or sea warfare which may affect the civilian population, individual civilians or civilian objects on land. They further apply to all attac·:s from the sea or from the air against objectives on land but do not otherwise affect the rules of international law applicable in armed conflict at sea or in the air.

4. The provisions of this Section are additional to the rules concerning humanitarian protection contained in the Fourth [Geneva] Convention [of 1949], particularly in Part II thereof, and in other international agreements binding upon the High Contracting Parties, as well as to other rules of international law relating to the protection of civilians and civilian objects on land, at sea or in the air against the effects of hostilities.

• • •

Article 52—General protection of civilian objects

1. Civilian objects shall not be the object of attack or of reprisals. Civilian objects are all objects which are not military objectives as defined in paragraph 2.

2. Attacks shall be limited strictly to military objectives. In so far as objects are concerned, military objectives are limited to those objects which by their nature, location, purpose or use make an effective contribution to military action and whose total or

partial destruction, capture or neutralization, in the circumstances ruling at the time, offers a definite military advantage.

3. In case of doubt whether an object which is normally dedicated to civilian purposes, such as a place of worship, a house or other dwelling or a school, is being used to make an effective contribution to military action, it shall be presumed not to be so used.

• • •

Article 54—Protection of objects indispensable to the survival of the civilian population

1. Starvation of civilians as a method of warfare is prohibited.

2. It is prohibited to attack, destroy, remove or render useless objects indispensable to the survival of the civilian population, such as foodstuffs, agricultural areas for the production of foodstuffs, crops, livestock, drinking water installations and supplies and irrigation works, for the specific purpose of denying them for their sustenance value to the civilian population or to the adverse Party, whatever the motive, whether in order to starve out civilians, to cause them to move away, or for any other motive.

3. The prohibitions in paragraph 2 shall not apply to such of the objects covered by it as are used by an adverse Party:

(*a*) as sustenance solely for the members of its armed forces; or

(*b*) if not as sustenance, then in direct support of military action, provided, however, that in no event shall actions against these objects be taken which may be expected to leave the civilian population with such inadequate food or water as to cause its starvation or force its movement.

4. These objects shall not be made the object of reprisals.

5. In recognition of the vital requirements of any Party to the conflict in the defence of its national territory against invasion, derogation from the prohibitions contained in paragraph 2 may be made by a Party to the conflict within such territory under its own control where required by imperative military necessity.

Article 55—Protection of the natural environment

1. Care shall be taken in warfare to protect the natural environment against widespread, long-term and severe damage. This protection includes a prohibition of the use of methods or means of warfare which are intended or may be expected to cause such damage to the natural environment and thereby to prejudice the health or survival of the population. [See also article 35.3.]

2. Attacks against the natural environment by way of reprisals are prohibited.

Article 56—Protection of works and installations containing dangerous forces

1. Works or installations containing dangerous forces, namely dams, dykes and nuclear electrical generating stations, shall not be made the object of attack, even where these objects are military objectives, if such attack may cause the release of dangerous forces and consequent severe losses among the civilian population. Other military objectives located at or in the vicinity of these works or installations shall not be made the object of attack if such attack may cause the release of dangerous forces from the works or installations and consequent severe losses among the civilian population.

2. The special protection against attack provided by paragraph 1 shall cease:

(*a*) for a dam or a dyke only if it is used for other than its normal function and in regular, significant and direct support of military operations and if such attack is the only feasible way to terminate such support;

(b) for a nuclear electrical generating station only if it provides electric power in regular, significant and direct support of military operations and if such attack is the only feasible way to terminate such support;

(c) for other military objectives located at or in the vicinity of these works or installations only if they are used in regular, significant and direct support of military operations and if such attack is the only feasible way to terminate such support.

3. In all cases, the civilian population and individual civilians shall remain entitled to all the protection accorded them by international law, including the protection of the precautionary measures provided for in Article 57. If the protection ceases and any of the works, installations or military objectives mentioned in paragraph 1 is attacked, all practical precautions shall be taken to avoid the release of the dangerous forces.

4. It is prohibited to make any of the works, installations or military objectives mentioned in paragraph 1 the object of reprisals.

5. The Parties to the conflict shall endeavour to avoid locating any military objectives in the vicinity of the works or installations mentioned in paragraph 1. Nevertheless, installations erected for the sole purpose of defending the protected works or installations from attack are permissible and shall not themselves be made the object of attack, provided that they are not used in hostilities except for defensive actions necessary to respond to attacks against the protected works or installations and that their armament is limited to weapons capable only of repelling hostile action against the protected works or installations.

6. The High Contracting Parties and the Parties to the conflict are urged to conclude further agreements among themselves to provide additional protection for objects containing dangerous forces.

7. In order to facilitate the identification of the objects protected by this article, the Parties to the conflict may mark them with a special sign consisting of a group of three bright orange circles placed on the same axis, as specified in Article 16 of Annex I to this Protocol. The absence of such marking in no way relieves any Party to the conflict of its obligations under this Article.

Article 57—Precautions in attack

1. In the conduct of military operations, constant care shall be taken to spare the civilian population, civilians and civilian objects.

2. With respect to attacks, the following precautions shall be taken:

(a) those who plan or decide upon an attack shall:

(i) do everything feasible to verify that the objectives to be attacked are neither civilians nor civilian objects and are not subject to special protection but are military objectives within the meaning of paragraph 2 of Article 52 and that it is not prohibited by the provisions of this Protocol to attack them;

(ii) take all feasible precautions in the choice of means and methods of attack with a view to avoiding, and in any event to minimizing, incidental loss of civilian life, injury to civilians and damage to civilian objects;

(iii) refrain from deciding to launch any attack which may be expected to cause incidental loss of civilian life, injury to civilians, damage to civilian objects, or a combination thereof, which would be excessive in relation to the concrete and direct military advantage anticipated;

(b) an attack shall be cancelled or suspended if it becomes apparent that the objective is not a military one or is subject to special protection or that the attack may be expected to cause incidental loss of civilian life, injury to civilians, damage to civilian objects, or a combination thereof, which would be excessive in relation to the concrete and direct military advantage anticipated;

(c) effective advance warning shall be given of attacks which may affect the civilian population, unless circumstances do not permit.

3. When a choice is possible between several military objectives for obtaining a similar military advantage, the objective to be selected shall be that the attack on which may be expected to cause the least danger to civilian lives and to civilian objects.

4. In the conduct of military operations at sea or in the air, each Party to the conflict shall, in conformity with its rights and duties under the rules of international law applicable in armed conflict, take all reasonable precautions to avoid losses of civilian lives and damage to civilian objects.

5. No provision of this Article may be construed as authorizing any attacks against the civilian population, civilians or civilian objects.

• • •

II. Parties

As of January 1984, the Geneva Protocol I of 1977 has accumulated a total of 37 parties. Of the five permanent members of the United Nations Security Council, so far only China has become a party, whereas France, the UK, the USA and the USSR have not. A list of all 37 parties of the Protocol as of January 1984, together with their year of joining, follows (ICRC, 1984):

Austria (1982), Bangladesh (1980), Bahamas (1980), Bolivia (1983), Botswana (1979), China (1983), Congo (1983), Costa Rica (1983), Cuba (1982), Cyprus (1979), Denmark (1982), Ecuador (1979), El Salvador (1978), Finland (1980), Gabon (1980), Ghana (1978), Jordan (1979), Korea, Rep. (1982), Libya (1978), Laos (1980), Mauritania (1980), Mauritius (1982), Mexico (1983), Mozambique (1983), Niger (1979), Norway (1981), St Lucia (1982), St Vincent & Grenadines (1983), Sweden (1979), Switzerland (1982), Syria (1983), Tanzania (1983), Tunisia (1979), United Arab Emirates (1983), Viet Nam (1981), Yugoslavia (1979), and Zaire (1982).

References

ICRC (International Committee of the Red Cross). 1984. States parties to the Geneva Conventions of 12 August 1949; states parties to the Protocols of 8 June 1977: as at 31 December 1983. *International Review of the Red Cross*, Geneva, **1984** (238): 26–29.

Roberts, A. and Guelff, R. (eds). 1982. *Documents on the Laws of War*. Oxford: Clarendon Press, 498 pp.

Index

releasing nitrogen oxides 17–18
Nuclear winter 5, 33
Nuremburg judgement 34–5, 37, 42

Partial Nuclear Test Ban Treaty,
 1963 66
Permafrost
 manipulation 6
 modification 69
 soils 29–30
Planets 3
Polar ice caps, melting 29
Polar ice cover 14–15
Prairie ecosystems 8
Precipitation, control 5

Radio communications, ionosphere 4
Radioactive contamination, effects of
 bombing 7
Radioactive fallout 58
Radioactivity, release 84
Rain-making 5, 13, 69, 79
Rainfall 18–20
 deprivation 19
 enhancement 19
Reagan, Ronald 35
Remote sensing 71, 74
Rivers, containment systems 28–29

Oceans, manipulation 7–8, 15
Oil tankers, destruction 9
Oil wells, destruction 9
Outer Space Treaty, 1967 10
Ozone layer
 penetration 4–5
 stratosphere 20–1

SALT agreements 66
San Andreas fault 26
Sea level, effects of polar ice cap
 melting 29
Seabed Treaty, 1971 10, 71
Second Indochina War 5, 8, 13, 19, 34,
 37, 39, 69, 79
Sino-Japanese War, 1937–45 6
Smog formation 18
Snow, making 69
Sovereign states, intervention in
 international affairs 41–2
Soviet Union *see* USSR
Space 3–4
Stars 3, 5
States, liability for extra-territorial
 effects 58

Storms, steering 69
Stratosphere 4
 modifiction 20–1
Sulphate particles, stratospheric ozone
 layers 21
Sulphur dioxide, atmospheric 17
Sun 3
Sweden 69

Thixotropic soils, fluidization 27–28
Troposphere 4
 gaseous composition 16–18
 modification 16–20
Tsunamis, generation 8, 26–27
Tundra ecosystems 8–9
 disruption 29–30

Ultraviolet radiation, release from ozone
 layer 4–5
United Kingdom 60
United Nations Charter 35, 60, 61
United Nations Conference on the
 Human Environment, 1972 37, 44,
 46, 88
United Nations Environment
 Programme 59, 88
United Nations General Assembly 38,
 42
United Nations Security Council 60, 62
United Nations War Crimes
 Commission 34–5, 37, 42
USA 35, 39, 40, 53, 54, 55, 56, 60, 65,
 69, 78, 79
USSR 53, 54, 56, 57, 60, 78

Veldt, burning 8
Verification
 Enmod Convention 59–61, 65–76
 international law of war 34
Volcanoes
 activation 28
 eruption 21

War, international law 33–44
Water, release 83–4
Weather, effects of nuclear war 5
Weather modification, secret war
 scenario 77–80
Winds, control 5
World Charter for Nature, 1982 10, 38,
 42, 44, 88
World Meteorological Organization 59

107